KRAV MAGA

REAL WORLD SOLUTIONS TO REAL WORLD VIOLENCE

T0151043

GERSHON BEN KEREN

TUTTLE Publishing

Tokyo | Rutland, Vermont | Singapore

This book is dedicated to Dennis Hanover, the "Survival Family," and the people of Israel

Published by Tuttle Publishing, an imprint of Periplus Editions (HK) Ltd.

www.tuttlepublishing.com

Copyright © 2014 Gershon Ben Keren

Library of Congress Cataloging-in-Publication Data
Ben Keren, Gershon.
  Krav Maga : real world solutions to real world violence / Gershon Ben Keren. -- First edition.
     pages cm
ISBN 978-0-8048-4392-8 (paperback -- ISBN 978-1-4629-1619-1 (ebook) 1. Krav maga. I. Title.
  GV1111.K43 2014
  796.81--dc23
                              2014030052

Distributed by:

North America, Latin America & Europe
Tuttle Publishing
364 Innovation Drive
North Clarendon, VT 05759-9436 U.S.A.
Tel: (802) 773-893; Fax: (802) 773-6993
info@tuttlepublishing.com
www.tuttlepublishing.com

Japan
Tuttle Publishing
Yaekari Building, 3rd Floor
5-4-12 Osaki, Shinagawa-ku
Tokyo 141 0032
Tel: (81) 3 5437-0171; Fax: (81) 3 5437-0755
sales@tuttle.co.jp
www.tuttle.co.jp

Asia Pacific
Berkeley Books Pte. Ltd.
61 Tai Seng Avenue #02-12
Singapore 534167
Tel: (65) 6280-1330; Fax: (65) 6280-6290
inquiries@periplus.com.sg
www.periplus.com

ISBN 978-0-8048-4392-8

First edition
18 17 16 15   6 5 4 3 2

Printed in Malaysia   1505TWP

TUTTLE PUBLISHING® is a registered trademark of Tuttle Publishing, a division of Periplus Editions (HK) Ltd.

Contents

Part 2: Self-Defense Scenarios

Part 3: Unarmed Assaults and Dynamic Components of Violence

Preface

I am foremost a martial artist. I say this because many people are under the impression that Krav Maga is little more than a collection of self-defense techniques that stresses function over form. Depending on the audience being taught, this may be the case—if you have three days to train a military unit who is getting ready to deploy, you are not going to spend time teaching them all of the subtleties and nuances of striking, blocking, etc. You are going to teach them the fundamentals, and rely on aggression and determination to fill the gap. However, where there is the opportunity to devote a longer period of time to training, then effort can be spent learning how to strike more efficiently, to move more effectively, and to place yourself in more advantageous positions, etc. This is where Krav Maga starts to become more than simply a military combatant system, and progresses towards being a full-fledged martial art.

I am a strong believer in the development of fighting skills and attributes, rather than simply learning techniques. If you are unfortunate enough to be attacked by a knife-wielding assailant, it is not your knowledge of a technique that will allow you to successfully defend yourself, but your ability to control range, dictate the movement of the fight, and have the necessary speed, movement, and timing to block, control, and dispatch your assailant. Too many times people believe in their ability to defend themselves because they "know" the appropriate technique to do so. This book contains the techniques—the knowledge—but to use it successfully, everything in it must be practiced, and then tested under high stress and duress.

My choice of techniques to present was based on the desire to explain some of the fundamentals of the Krav Maga system I teach, and show certain ideas which are contained in it; such as the reuse of movements, and the similarities between dealing with knife and gun. I describe some of the dynamics and situational components of violence so that you can gain a better idea of what real world violence looks like. I am also a great believer that much of the violence that targets the individual can be predicted, identified, and avoided—and I have tried to bring this out in some of the scenarios that are described.

When we shot the photographs for the book, we made the decision to shoot them in real time, as we wanted to express the movement and dynamism that exists in a real life conflict. This process involve photographing techniques demonstrated at full pace, and full force, over and over again, and then selecting individual photographs from the over 10,000 that we took, to get "snapshot" moments that illustrated a particular part of the technique. None of the photos you see in the book were staged, or performed statically. As painful and as time consuming as this process was, I believe it gives a much better idea of what violence and the responses to it look like, as well as allowing you to have faith and conviction that the techniques described actually work.

We also made the decision to try to shoot, where possible, in the situations/scenarios where certain assaults and threats are likely to occur, e.g., at ATMs, in bars, etc. This will help you visualize the techniques and the attacks more clearly, and give a more realistic context to them.

Krav Maga Yashir is a systematic approach to self-defense, not merely an encyclopedia of techniques. There are common movements, ideas, and principles that are shared by every technique in the system. If you truly understand one technique, you understand them all, and by understanding them, you will be able to create solutions and responses to attacks that you have never trained for or experienced before. This, for me, is the pinnacle of Krav Maga training.

I am a full time Krav Maga instructor, and there are very few days when I am not on the mats teaching and/or training. The system I teach continues—and will always continue—to evolve, and I am grateful to my instructors in Israel and in the U.S., who continue to extend my experiences and knowledge, so that I can better provide my students with the solutions that they need to survive real world violence. My hope is that this book will go a long way towards communicating this same teaching, and that it will improve your survival chances should you ever find yourself in a potentially violent situation.

OSS/Respect
Gershon Ben Keren

Introduction

What Is Krav Maga?

Krav Maga, meaning "Contact Combat," is a method of fighting taught to soldiers and military personnel by the IDF (Israeli Defense Forces). It is a proven method of self-defense that has been tested to be effective in one of the toughest and most hostile environments on the planet: Israel and the Middle East.

Using natural reflexive actions to deal with threats and attacks, Krav Maga works with the way your body will naturally respond when subjected to the high stress and elevated emotions that are part of a violent confrontation. The training is based on what you will do when assaulted, not what you think you will do, or would think you should do. Techniques and solutions that deal with one problem/attack are reused to deal with others, thus reducing the total number of techniques that need to be learned and trained.

Krav Maga techniques are simple, brutal, and no-nonsense, with no regard to aesthetics. They are 100 percent utilitarian in nature and are designed to be performed effectively in any emotional state—whether you are tired, surprised, or stressed, etc. Krav Maga never assumes a state of preparedness (there are even training stances that reflect this lack of readiness).

It doesn't matter if you are standing, sitting down, laying down or in any other physical position—Krav Maga teaches you to fight from where you are, not where you would ideally want to be. It teaches defensive tactics against both unarmed and armed assailants, as well as against multiple attackers. No possible scenario is ever excluded or discounted when training solutions to violence—if it can happen, it's trained.

Krav Maga teaches a "survival" mindset of never giving up, however insurmountable the odds against you may seem. In the IDF, the system has one goal: To get a new recruit combat-ready, both emotionally and physically, in the shortest possible time.

Krav Maga is constantly evolving, simplifying, and improving techniques, developing and evolving new ones, and making others redundant and obsolete. This makes it the most up to date and relevant system of self-defense available.

Based on systematic concepts and principles, Krav Maga teaches the practitioner how to think, understand, and assess a situation dynamically, and to choose existing techniques to deal with a problem, or create "new" solutions as necessary. It is not just about learning and memorizing techniques, but empowering the individual to act as the situation dictates. This makes Krav Maga a realistic system of self-defense that can be used by civilians, law enforcement officials, and military personnel to deal with any potential threat, attack, or violent situation in which they may find themselves.

Krav Maga Yashir

Krav Maga is an umbrella term that is used to refer to a variety of fighting systems that adhere to the concepts and principles first laid out by Imi Lichtenfeld in the 1940s. Krav Maga systems are not so much defined by their techniques (as different units within the IDF may have different responsibilities and remits) as by the principles upon which these techniques are founded. This means that while different Krav Maga systems may share similar techniques, they may also include significantly different ones—and also teach different solutions to the same situation, depending on various situational factors.

Krav Maga Yashir (*Yashir* meaning "direct" or "straight" in Hebrew) is a system of fighting and self-defense based on the blueprint that Imi Lichtenfeld first laid down in the 1930s and 1940s. It operates according to the five basic principles that are shared by all Krav Maga systems:

- Attack should be as close to defense as possible.
- Make yourself safe before attacking.
- Movements should be instinctive and reflexive.
- Attacks should focus on vulnerable target areas, e.g., eyes, throat, groin, etc.
- Use the environment to assist in your defense/attack.

These common Krav Maga principles are the foundation of certain distinct concepts that are used within the Krav Maga Yashir system (and that will be referred back to and elaborated throughout the book):

- Action is Preferable to Reaction
- Disrupt, Damage, Destroy, and Disengage
- Every Defense is an Attack
- Control the Environment, not the Individual
- Assume the Assailant is Armed, Assisted, and Able

Action is always preferable to reaction—it is always preferable to be the assailant rather than the victim. If violence is inevitable, then it is better to be the person initiating the assault rather than receiving it (when first hit, most people will crumble emotionally—you want this to be your assailant rather than yourself). If you miss, or are denied, the opportunity to make a preemptive assault, and are therefore assaulted, your first step must be to disrupt your assailant's initial attack, preventing them the opportunity to follow it up. You must next look to inflict damage on them before destroying them and/or disengaging. No movement you make should ever be seen as purely defensive. If you have to block an assailant's strike, your block should be looked on as an offensive response that can cause pain or damage to your attacker. This could act as a disruption to their attack, giving you the opening to launch your own damaging strikes—attack should be as close to defense as possible.

Aggressive and violent confrontations don't happen in a vacuum, they happen in an environment that has objects in it that you can use, both as weapons and as barriers. The environment will also contain objects that can be used against you, and possibly other individuals that can cause you harm. A fight is not just about you and the individual you face, but about everything else within the environment. At the same time, you should never underestimate the primary assailant you face, and should assume that they are both armed and able to deal with you.

The Krav Maga Yashir system takes this situational approach to dealing with violence and trains it accordingly, putting attacks and threats into their appropriate contexts and altering situational components—such as location, assailant motive, relationship with the assailant, etc.—to demonstrate how these components can alter the solutions you choose to use. This book will describe and demonstrate Krav Maga techniques within this context, not just showing how a particular technique should be performed, but also how the attack or assault developed and was carried out, and which non-physical solutions could have been put in place to avoid having been targeted in the first place.

The book is organized into three parts. The first looks at the basic fighting skills you need to develop in order to survive a violent confrontation (how to move, position yourself, block and strike, etc.); the second part describes various armed and unarmed assaults and the situations in which they occur; while the third part looks at some of the dynamic factors that can occur within a fight, such as being caught in a headlock, ending up in a clinch, etc., and how to deal with this.

Gershon Ben Keren

The Krav Maga Yashir system was developed by Gershon Ben Keren, a Krav Maga instructor who has spent the past 20 years training with a variety of Krav Maga and military trainers in Israel, and in 2010 was inducted into the Museum of the History of Martial Arts in Israel by Dr. Dennis Hanover (founder of Dennis Hisardut). He also holds a 2nd Degree Black Belt in Kodokan Judo, and a 1st Degree Black Belt in Kosen Judo. Gershon Ben Keren has an academic background in Psychology, with particular regard to aggression and violence. He combines this with his experiences in the security industry to present Krav Maga in a contextualized way, rather than by simply demonstrating/explaining physical techniques. The system referred to in this book is the product of Ben Keren's training and reflects the different approaches that various IDF instructors have taken in teaching Krav Maga. The strength of the Krav Maga Yashir system is that it is influenced by the experiences and teachings of several different senior IDF instructors and trainers, and builds on their combined experiences and approaches, rather than simply reflecting the ideas and methods of one.

The system looks to stay true to the principles, concepts, and ideas first laid down by Imi Lichtenfeld, while at the same time looking to incorporate the teaching and training methods of more traditional martial arts. Krav Maga Yashir is also influenced by modern security training protocols, advocated by various military, law enforcement and private security agencies.

PART 1

Basic Skills (Stances, Movement, Blocking, and Striking)

Stances and Movement

A street fight is not a fight, it is an assault. Nobody who attacks you actually wants to fight; they merely want a victim that they can physically punish, rape, or steal from. A "fight" would imply that an aggressor wants to give you the opportunity to participate and "fight back"—but no aggressor wants to be met with resistance. This is the reality of violence. This is why real world violence differs so markedly from combat sports and sparring, which are voluntary (and controlled) acts of violence, in which both participants willingly agree to engage. Real life violence is something that is forced upon you, not something you consent to—usually in locations and situations which are designed to inhibit your movement and ability to disengage and which are advantageous to your assailant.

The only time that you will have the opportunity to adopt a stance is when you have picked up on any available pre-violence indicators in the situation, such as a person moving towards you in a purposeful and aggressive manner, or someone becoming verbally abusive towards you. You will be able to adopt an Interview Stance, for example, in the Pre-Conflict phase of violence (see below).

The Timeline of Violence

*All violence happens along a timeline and can be broken down into five distinct phases: The **Non-Conflict** phase is one where there is no sign of harmful intent in the environment; the **Conflict-Aware** phase is where you initially become adrenalized, but have not yet ascertained if the danger is directed towards you; the **Pre-Conflict** phase is where you have recognized and assessed that an aggressor's harmful intent is* *towards you but they haven't yet made a physical assault, e.g., they may be verbally abusive towards you; the* **Conflict** *phase is the assault itself; and the* **Post-Conflict** *phase is everything that occurs once the assault has ended (such as disengaging to safety as well as seeking medical attention, getting legal advice, etc.).*

The Interview Stance

Most violent encounters involve a verbal confrontation that precedes any physical assault. Depending on the motive of the aggressor and their emotional state, it may be possible to de-escalate the situation and resolve the conflict without having to engage with them physically.

An aggressor's body language and their ability to communicate verbally will indicate whether they are about to launch an assault. If they respond to a question such as, "What can I do to sort this situation out?" with silence, with jumbled up words, or by simply repeating their complaint over and over again, you should take this as an indication that they are about to make an attack.

The point of the Interview Stance is to get you into a physically strong position, while at the same time not appearing overly aggressive—you don't want to escalate the situation at this point by giving your aggressor a reason to pull a knife, gun, or other weapon. Neither do you want to appear overly timid or fearful. Instead, you want to communicate through your body language that you don't want any trouble, but at the same time you are confident in your ability to handle any attack. Your goal should always be to avoid a physical confrontation, and if you can, you should either try to discourage your assailant from attacking or de-escalate the situation. You should also put yourself in a position to be able to make a preemptive assault if you recognize that a physical confrontation is inevitable because you were unable to de-escalate or disengage from the situation.

Key Points Regarding the Interview Stance

The aim of the Interview Stance is twofold: firstly, it should present you in a non-threatening way to your aggressor, and secondly, it should prepare you for a physical confrontation. If a person is verbally aggressive towards you, you don't want to escalate the situation by balling your fists and trying to intimidate them—if they are carrying a weapon, such as a gun or knife, they may feel that your aggressive posture necessitates them pulling their weapon (once somebody pulls a weapon it is very unlikely that they will put it away without using it). Your goal should be to present yourself in a non-threatening, but confident way. Your aggressor is probably used to people either cowering or posturing back when threatened, so presenting them with a different image can cause them to question the situation.

Your head should be directly over your hips, so you are stable. If your head moves forward or backwards from this position you may still be "balanced," but you won't be stable, and this increases the risk of you being taken to ground. Your arms should protect the space in front of you, creating a "No Man's Land" that your assailant's strikes would have to cross to reach you.

You should appear non-threatening but in control. By using a hand gesture (open palm facing forward) that is the international signal for both "Stop" and "I don't want any trouble," you are sending a confusing message to your aggressor. When this is coupled with an upright and "dominant" posture, you are presenting yourself in a way that most assailants are not used to being met with, i.e., you are not cowering or acting submissively, but at the same time you are not acting aggressively or appearing to posture back. You are also in an excellent position to both defend yourself physically and launch any necessary preemptive assaults. Obviously if you are attacked by surprise then you will not have time to adopt such a stance; however, if somebody verbally threatens you or acts in a manner that makes you uncomfortable, this should be your first response.

1. The foot of your least dominant hand should be the one you lead with. This keeps your dominant hand at the rear, from where it is able to generate the most power (for ease of communication, the techniques in this book will default to right hand dominance going forward).

2. Your feet should be on opposite corners of an imaginary rectangle, with your toes pointing towards your assailant—the feet control the direction of your hips, and it is the movement of your hips which will give power to your striking. This stance will also make you stable in all but two directions, meaning that if you are knocked from the front, side, or rear (you must always assume that there is more than one attacker), you will be able to stay on your feet.

3. Your head must be over your hips. Your head controls the direction of your weight, and if you are leaning forward or backwards you can easily be thrown off-balance in those directions. For the same reason, your weight must be evenly distributed between both feet. Make sure you hold your head upright and stand tall, so that you appear confident and in control.

4. Both legs should remain active. That is, they should be able to create movement without having to shift weight first. Keep the knees bent and the legs relaxed, so that they don't have to be unlocked in order for you to move.

5. Your weight should be on your toes. Toes are for moving, heels are for braking. Don't lift the heels of your feet too high, as when you move you will want to make sure that they can be placed down quickly if necessary, e.g., to be able to strike with power.

6. Your hands should be placed out in front of you, with the palms of your hands facing your aggressor. Unlike clenched fists, this hand position is non-aggressive, and is understood in all cultures to be a non-threatening gesture. It is also the international sign for "stop" and "stay back."

Controlling Range

If you are too close to a potential assailant, they will be able to strike or grab you without having to make any prior body movement. Therefore, you should always keep a suitable distance between yourself and your assailant, forcing them to have to move before they make an attack. If they make a movement forward, to move into attacking range, you should make a corresponding movement backwards or away, to maintain your original distance. If you don't, and you stay within their range, you will be attempting to counter the speed of their arm/punch, rather than the relatively slower speed of their body. In most cases action beats reaction, so you will be unsuccessful in countering their attack if you don't force them to reposition their body, first.

Forcing them to move their body before making an attack will give you a larger movement to respond to, rather than having to react to somebody's arm speed. If they can punch or grab you without having to move first, you are limiting your chances of identifying the attack.

When you face someone who is acting aggressively towards you, you should attempt to control the range. You want to position yourself at a distance where, if they want to strike or grab you, they must move their body into range first. This larger body movement is easier to detect than an arm movement alone.

If an assailant is already in range, they can punch you or grab you without having to make any prior body movement. In this instance, you will have to react to the arm movement alone, which is a much faster and smaller movement than that of the body coming forwards—and so much harder to detect and respond to.

The simplest way to learn how to control range—before it becomes an inherent fighting skill—is to make sure that when you look at the center of your aggressor's chest, you are able to see some of the ground or floor in front of their forward foot with your peripheral vision. If the person is holding a knife, you need to roughly add the length of the blade to this distance, as the length of the weapon will give them a greater range (than a fist alone).

You need to be close enough for them to believe that they can, with one movement, reach you. If you are too far away they will simply close the distance on you first before making an assault. If violence is inevitable, you need to draw out your assailant's attack in such a way that it will commit them to their attack, and put them in a disadvantageous position.

This control of range should force them to commit all their weight forward when they make an attack. With their weight forward, they are both vulnerable to a counterattack, and at the same time slowed down in making further attacks, as they will have to readjust their weight to do so.

Relative Body Positioning

Aside from controlling range, you should also attempt to control your assailant's movement by continually moving offline. Power is derived from the hips, and people are at their strongest when their hips are lined up facing you—this is also a position which allows them to step directly towards you and take advantage of this movement of mass to add power to their strikes.

When you stand directly in front of an assailant, you are facing all of their "weapons" (hands, feet, knees, etc.) in a position where they are able to deliver strikes with full power. You should always avoid facing an assailant's hips (the source of power in striking).

By moving off at an angle, you are getting "offline," while at the same time forcing your attacker to turn towards you before making an attack. At the moment they turn, they are vulnerable to any attack you may make. You are also forcing them to take an extra step before they can assault you, slowing down their attack.

Maintain your control of range as you turn, so that your assailant is unable to reach you without moving...

...This forces them to move, as well as having to turn, slowing down their attack and giving you a lot of time to respond, either by blocking their attack, or making your own while they do this.

You should always try to force your assailant to do several things before they can attack you:
1. Shift weight before they can turn their body;
2. Physically turn towards you;
3. Take a step towards you.
If at the same time you only have to do one thing, i.e., attack them, while they complete all of these actions, you should always be faster than your assailant.

If you move offline, you are no longer directly in front of your aggressor. This means that in order to attack you, they must shift and readjust their weight and then turn so that they are facing you again. Relative Body Positioning combined with range control means that an assailant must do three things before they can assault you:

1. Shift their body weight before re-aligning their body.
2. Realign their body before moving.
3. Move towards you before being able to attack.

Whoever controls the movement of the fight, controls the fight. You should move in such a way that it is difficult for your attacker to synchronize their movement to yours. If you keep moving to your left, for example, your attacker will eventually realize that the next time you move, it will be to your left, and attack you as you move there. Move in an unpredictable fashion.

Violence is dynamic, and you should always be moving, whether it is before the fight or during it—you should never be a fixed, static target. If you're not moving, you're not fighting. Your movement should always accomplish at least one of the following three things. If it isn't doing so, you are moving without purpose:

1. Your movement should be away from danger.
2. Your movement should be part of an attack/assault.
3. Your movement should create an attacking opportunity.

Ideally, every time you move you should be creating attacking opportunities, or be attacking. If you move defensively it should be to a position from which you can attack. Every movement in Krav Maga should either be an attack, or one that facilitates an attack. Being defensively minded is no way to deal with an attacker.

Relative Body Positioning with Multiple Assailants

Always assume your assailant is armed (even if you can't see a weapon, or have disarmed them of one), always assume they are as good as you, and always assume that they have third parties nearby who can come to their assistance.

It would be wrong for us to assume a fight simply involves one attacker. A fight is about controlling everything in the environment, including entrance/exit routes, objects that can be used as weapons, objects that can be used as barriers and obstacles, along with any other individuals with us, and/or individuals who may assist our primary aggressor.

If you are dealing with an aggressor, either verbally or physically, you should assume that any movement coming towards you is aggressive in nature. Don't assume it is somebody about to intervene on your behalf, e.g., a friend, a security person, etc. Your job is to "line them up," so you are only facing one person at a time.

If the third party/secondary assailant tries to move round the person in front of you, you should move so that you keep them directly behind the primary aggressor.

Once your assailants are lined up, you should do everything you can to maintain this structure. In a physical confrontation, your goal should be to take the person who is directly in front of you out of the fight as quickly as possible, then face the next attacker and do the same, until all assailants are dealt with.

Focusing and dealing with one person at a time, when possible, is a much more effective strategy than moving between multiple attackers with your assaults. Concentrate force on each one in turn, taking them out of the fight one by one.

When you move you should scan and look around, to get an understanding of your environment. Are there objects you can use as weapons? Objects you can use as barriers, such as cars or tables? Are there people moving towards you? Uninvolved people usually move away from confrontations, not towards them, so someone moving towards you and your assailant should be seen as another potential threat—don't assume it is someone coming to help you.

If you are dealing with multiple assailants, or can see people coming towards you, you do not want to be caught in the middle of them—rather, you should line them up so you are only facing one person at a time. This person will act as the pivot point of the group—as the others try to reach you, you will keep them in line by moving in the same direction, around the central person you've selected to deal with first. If you are in a situation where you have a choice of who that person is, you should choose to face the most aggressive first, as they will definitely want to be involved in the fight. Choosing to deal with a less aggressive person, who may have been content to stay out of the fight, will mean that you will have to deal with both of them, when it could have been just the primary aggressor.

How to Move

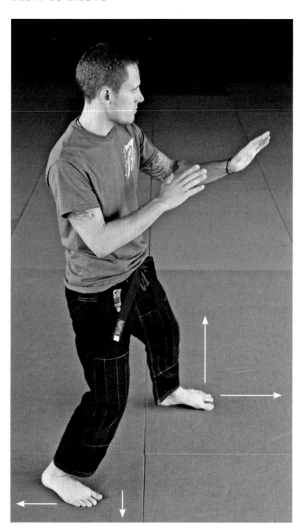

To move backwards, move the rear foot first, followed by the front foot.

To move left, move the left foot first, followed by right foot.

To move forward, move the forward foot first, followed by the rear foot.

To move right, move the right foot first, followed by the left foot.

Your feet should always slide and feel a connection with the floor, rather than stepping. This will prevent you from putting your foot down on something unstable or slippery. If you slide and transfer your weight in a controlled fashion, you will be able to feel whether or not what is beneath your feet is solid and can be trusted to bear your weight. Stepping actions also demonstrate to your assailant a transfer of weight—if they are trained, they will be able to exploit this by easily sweeping your feet.

When you want to move forward, simply move the forward foot, sliding it about a foot's length, plant it, and bring the rear foot up so you are in the same stance as you were before. It should be the rear foot pushing the body which initiates the body and forward foot to move. As you move forward, be careful to keep your weight over your hips, rather than overly transferring it to the front foot. This transference could make you vulnerable to being swept before you place the foot down, it could also make your front leg a solid target for a kick, as it will be too rooted and unable to ride the movement of any strike to it.

If you want to move backwards, repeat this process in reverse, pushing off with the front foot and sliding the rear foot, again keeping the weight centered. Every time you move, you should find yourself back in your original stance (feet on opposite corners of a rectangle, weight distributed 50/50, both legs active).

When you move either to the left or right, the same rules apply. When you move to the left, you should push off with the right foot, slide the left foot to the left, and resume your stance. Moving to the right will involve force being applied by the left foot to allow the right to slide first.

Other Stances

If you are attacked without warning (most assaults are preceded by a verbal exchange), your hands may be down (we call this "Unprepared Stance"), halfway up ("Semi-Prepared Stance") or in some other position; equally, your footing may be unbalanced and your body alignment off. It is important to train from these unprepared and semi-prepared positions, and to practice taking the first opportunity in these situations to get into a stable stance from which you can strike.

Unprepared Stance—This is a training stance that is used to replicate our body/hand position when we are attacked by surprise. In Krav Maga, we don't assume we'll always be in a state of readiness when assaulted, and so train from positions of unreadiness, where our hands are down and our feet are not in the most stable position, etc.

We also train from positions where we are seated, walking, and even lying down.

Semi-Prepared Stance—There are times when we naturally react to movements (threatening and non-threatening) by bringing our hands up. It should also become a first response for us to start to bring our hands up as soon as we recognize that we are being assaulted.

The Semi-Prepared Stance is a training stance that acknowledges this natural reaction, from which we train the first moments of a physical confrontation.

Fighting Stance—This is a stance that demonstrates principles, such as keeping the hands up high when they are not being used to strike or block with. If you have the space and time to adopt a fighting stance in a real-life confrontation, you have either missed an opportunity to attack your assailant, or failed to disengage from them—otherwise you should be adopting an Interview Stance, with the goal of de-escalating the situation. Just as with the Interview Stance, your least dominant hand (and leg) should be forward. You should never find yourself in a static stance, as you should always be moving in a fight, either attacking, or preparing to attack.

Striking, Punching, Kicking, and Throwing

If you believe that violence is inevitable you should strike preemptively, rather than wait to be attacked. If you have adopted the Interview Stance and in talking to your assailant find them so aggressive and emotional that they don't respond, or you understand that their motive is one that will inevitably lead to physical violence (they have a pre-planned goal they wish to accomplish, such as an abduction or mugging), you should take control of the situation and attack first.

If disengagement is an option, and you can move behind a protective barrier such as a car and/or exit the situation, you should. If there is something in the environment you can use as a weapon then it would be advisable to arm yourself, for you should always assume that your assailant is armed, and you don't want to have to deal with them in this capacity without a weapon of your own.

Preemptive Striking Combination

Following is detailed a preemptive striking combination that all Krav Maga Yashir students learn. In reality, it can be dissected and any part of the combination can be used during any stage of a physical assault, not just at the beginning, or in the order shown here.

The combination leads with a preemptive strike. All the other techniques (the kick, the punches, the knee, etc.) flow out from there in an unbroken fashion, with each strike setting up the next. The body has three naturally weak targets that no amount of gym work and training can strengthen. These are the eyes, the throat, and the groin. A little force applied to each one of these targets will result in a great deal of pain and discomfort, which makes them excellent "first choice" targets.

*The Krav Maga Yashir system works along a continuum, referred to as **Disrupt, Damage, Destroy**, and **Disengage**. The first strike that is thrown should look to disrupt the assailant from either making an assault, or from continuing with their assault. To do this, you should attack the soft targets listed, with fast strikes that don't require any power to be effective. If you are assaulted when unprepared and surprised, it will take you a relatively long time to get into a position from which you can deliver powerful strikes. You will be able to create this time by disrupting your assailant with an eye, throat, or groin strike and follow these with power strikes, which you will use to finish the fight.*

Lead Eye Strike

A poor eye strike is much more effective than a poor punch, and so makes a very good initial strike. It also doesn't rely on "body power" to be effective, and can therefore be thrown from almost all body positions. Even if it doesn't land, it will normally cause the person receiving it to pull their head back, restricting their ability to make an attack (in that moment).

From the Interview Stance, turn on the toes of the front foot and extend your front hand, aiming your fingers at your assailant's eyes. The hand should flick out towards them, with the pivoting motion of the toes bringing the hip forward and turning the body, to give you a better reach. If your assailant is too far away for you to reach this way, you will need to take a small, sliding step forward to close the distance.

If your strike connects, it will cause your aggressor's eyes to water, disrupting them from making their own attack, and preventing them from defending themselves against your next, more damaging attack. Even if you don't make contact, this fast movement aimed at their eyes will cause them to blink or pull their head back, giving you an opening to move in with a hard strike.

Groin Kick

Depending on the position of your aggressor's stance, you may need to move before making the groin kick, as their leg position may prevent you from reaching your target.

Although extremely simple and effective, groin kicks can be relatively difficult to pull off in real life situations. This isn't because the kick is performed badly, but because people have a natural tendency to pull the hips back, and drop their hands to protect themselves when there is movement towards the groin. The groin is a relatively small and well-protected target.

Although groin strikes can be difficult to pull off, the effects of a good groin kick can be devastating—whether it is the instep of the foot or the shin that connects. Even if a connection is light—or possibly nonexistent—a person will pull their hips back in response, setting them up for other attacks, and putting them in a disadvantageous position.

If the person is standing square to you, simply pull back the hand that made the eye-strike (using the body/pull of the hip), and push the other hip forward, while raising the knee by pushing off from the toes of the rear foot. Then rapidly extend the foot—and shin—upwards into your attacker's groin. This is not a flick, it is a powerful kick, delivered with full force. You should lean back slightly as you make the kick, so your body and leg make a see-sawing movement over the hip.

Understand how one hip pulling back assists the other in coming forward, so that both hips are involved in the kick. This is how real power is generated. This double-hip motion is common to all Krav Maga Yashir power strikes, whether they are kicks, punches, hammerfists, or slaps.

If the person is standing with one leg forward, you will need to move to their opposite side in order to attack the groin—e.g., if they are standing with their left foot forward, you will need to move to their right (your left) in order to expose the groin.

Step out diagonally with your left foot, which will now position you offline from your assailant and them square to you, as if both legs were on the same line. As you take this step, deliver the kick.

Putting Your Assailant in a Disadvantaged Position
When an assailant facing you has one leg forward and the other back, they are in a relatively strong body position. If you can move to a point where your assailant's legs are spread out on a line directly in front of you, they are in a very weak position and are not particularly stable. If a person is leading with their left leg, stepping to your left will expose them this way, and vice versa, if they lead with their right leg you should move to your right.

If a person is standing before you with both legs spread wide, you can make a groin kick without having to change your body position. However, if they are standing with one leg forward, the groin will be protected and it will be necessary to move to a more accessible position first.

If the person's left leg is forward, you will need to move to your left, in order to expose their groin.

Push off with your right foot and take a sliding step to your left. The pushing off motion of the right foot will initiate the kicking action of the right leg (all kicks should start with a pushing motion from the floor).

Pull the heel of the right foot back towards your right buttock as you transfer all of your weight onto your left leg. At the same time, bring your arms across your body to maintain a high guard to protect yourself.

Once the heel has reached the buttock and can go no further, the snapping motion of the kick can begin. The toes should be pulled back, in order to protect them, and contact should be made with the instep of the foot or the shin. It is wise to aim with the lower shin, so if the person pulls back the hips further than anticipated, you will still be able to make contact with the instep.

Start to extend/straighten the leg, as you swing the shin/foot through towards the groin.

As you extend and straighten the leg you should push the hip forward into the strike—this will involve you leaning backwards somewhat. This added hip movement will give power to the kick, and help knock the arms away if the person has brought them down to defend themselves.

Whenever you kick, your supporting leg (in this example, the left) should always have a bend at the knee. This will allow you to straighten up, adding more "lift" to the kick, as well as allowing you to move after making the kick, without having to readjust your weight. This is something that is difficult to do with a straight leg, i.e., it would have to be bent first before it could move.

With the right amount of force delivered with the leg and hips, you should be able to "lift" the person up. This puts them in an extremely weak defensive position to deal with any follow up attacks you make (you should never rely on one strike to finish the fight).

Lead Hand Punches and Rear Crosses

As you bring the kicking leg back, return to your original stance, pull your hands back into a more defensive guard. This will not only put your hands in a better defensive position, but will also set them in a position from which you can deliver strong punches (keep your hands open, rather than in fists, as this will keep the arms relaxed and allow you to tighten your fist fully on impact).

The lead hand punch should be delivered with full force and commitment—it should not be considered as a "jab" or set-up punch, but one that has enough force to be effective in its own right.

A common expression in Israel regarding lead hand versus rear hand punches is, "hospital/graveyard," i.e., your lead hand punch should put your aggressor in the hospital, your rear hand punch in the graveyard. This is because a rear hand strike can harness the power of both hips and all of the back muscles, along with a complete transfer of weight, and has more space to accelerate.

Whenever you hit somebody with a closed fist, you are attempting to hit them with full force and power. There is never any point in throwing a punch if it doesn't contain power—and by power we mean all of the force that your body is able to generate. When a punch is thrown, it should not be done as a distracting or disrupting strike, but as a blow that will cause damage. In order for this to be effective, two things must first occur:

1. You must to be in an optimal position that will allow you to generate full and maximal power (you can use a strike to a soft target to get into such a position);

2. Your aggressor has to be in a disadvantaged position, where the full force of your strike will be felt (if you hit them as they are moving back, for example, the full force of your strike may be lost as it is translated into additional backwards movement, rather than being absorbed by their body). If you can attack them when their feet are planted on a straight line in front of you, they will be in a seriously disadvantaged position.

Starting from a fighting stance...

...Start to move your weight forward, pivoting on the toes.

Push the hip forward, and extend the arm (elbow tight).

Straighten the arm, and tighten/clench the fist.

Recoil the arm by pulling the left hip back.

At the same time drive the right hip and arm forward.

To attain full power with the rear hand punch, both hips have to be involved. The left hip should pull back from the lead hand strike and help push the right hip forward. This double hip motion, coupled with the engagement of the back muscles (notice how in the photo the torso is twisted somewhat), means that the whole upper body and hips are powering the punch. If the power of the right leg is added, pushing the body weight forward, the sheer amount of force generated can start to be appreciated. Whenever we strike with full force, all of our body should be utilized to generate maximum power.

By the time the arm is fully extended, your weight should have transferred to the point where 65–70 percent is on the forward leg and 30–35 percent on the rear leg. The head should still be over the hips, rather than leaning forward, with both front and rear legs bent. Your hips should have dropped and feel "heavy," while the feet should feel light (sinking the hips will also help you avoid over-reaching the strike and lifting the back foot off the ground). While full commitment must be given to the strike (both emotional and physical), you should still be able to move and readjust your body position without major readjustments in body weight first.

For any punch to contain real power:

1. Weight must transfer from the back leg to the forward leg.
2. The hips must turn (one pulling and the other pushing).
3. The back muscles must pull and engage to turn the upper body.
4. The shoulder of the striking hand must turn over.
5. The hand/fist/arm must time the transference of the power and momentum into the target.

It is important that all of your striking and movements have the feeling that it is the body that moves the arms, and not the arms or hands that lead the body. It is the body that propels the arm forward when punching, and the body that pulls it back when recoiling and re-setting the strike. The power of the punch comes from the synergy produced by combining the push of the rear leg with the turn of the hips, along with the pull of the back and the added rotation of the shoulder. The extension/straightening of the arm is merely the means of timing by which this power is transferred into the target.

From your stance, push off from the floor with your rear leg and start to shift your weight forward onto the front leg. At the same time, turn and pivot on the toes of your front foot, pushing your front hip forward and pulling your rear hip back. You should feel your hips sink as you do this—you want to feel heavy in the hips and light on your feet as you strike. As this is happening, your arm should begin to extend. You should extend the arm as if you had a wall on your left side preventing your elbow from moving outside of your "silhouette."

You should always try to strike out from the body in a way that doesn't cause your shape to change or "break." If you move your elbow later-ally away from your side, the shape that you present to your assailant will change, giving them advance warning of your punch. We refer to this as "Breaking Shape." To avoid this happening, we maintain the idea of keeping the silhouette our aggressor sees the same. Conversely, you should try to put your assailant in positions where they are forced to break their shape as part of their attack.

When striking/punching, we want to give as little warning as possible. To achieve this we want to change our body shape as little as possible. You can see in the following sequence that when an attacker throws a big "circular" strike, their whole body shape changes. First they pull back their striking arm—this is when you should start to respond.

Here, the attacker's shape has completely changed, or "broken," as their arm comes out to start the strike. Compare this with the minimal change in shape of the body in the sequence demonstrating "straight punches" (see pages 30–31).

Although big, circular strikes are extremely powerful, they are much easier to spot than straight strikes, as the body shape needs to change so much in order to deliver them. This is one of the reasons why, when we deliver straight strikes, we need to keep our elbows close to our body.

This position demonstrates the point where a block would have to intercept the punch. As you can see, there is a relatively long period of time, and several phases, before the punch gets to this point. This makes circular strikes much easier to deal with than straight punches. They are also much more common amongst untrained individuals.

By guarding our silhouette, i.e., putting our arms out in front of us (as in the Interview Stance), we make it difficult for assailants to deliver straight strikes/punches. This can force an attacker to throw circular strikes in order to hit us. Forcing our assailant to break shape in this way improves our chances of blocking their strikes.

As your arm extends, turn the shoulder, making sure that your shoulder isn't lifted/shrugged up. Don't lean into the strike, but rather keep your head over your hips and bend your knees slightly to drop your weight. When you judge that your strike will hit, tighten the fist. Make sure you throw your strike from a distance from which you can drive your punch through the target, rather than just connecting with it (this is not a "push," but a conscious delivery of power into your aggressor). As soon as you feel the power dissipate, recoil the strike.

The recoil is achieved by the body/hip pulling the strike back, not simply by bending the elbow and pulling the arm back.

As you pull the left hip back, shift the weight so that it is more evenly spread between your feet. At the same time, drive the right hip forward—pushing off from the ball of the right foot. As your right arm starts to pass your left arm, begin to extend it, making sure that you keep the elbow down. As it starts to close in on the target, rotate the fist so that the knuckles are up and the shoulder engages—just as with a lead straight punch, keep the shoulder down, seated in the socket. Just before your fist impacts into the target, clench it tightly.

Rear "Crashing" Elbow

To deliver a "crashing" elbow, recoil the right hand by pulling back the right hip. The hand and hip move together. The pull should be strong enough that you pivot on the left foot, as if you were throwing a lead hand punch. Once both hips have turned to face to the right and your weight is on your rear leg, unwind the hips towards your assailant, and start to transfer your weight forward (if your aggressor has moved back as a consequence of your punches, you may need to step forward to reach them—this movement can help you transfer weight forward). Make sure your head remains over your hips.

The body's most devastating natural weapons are the knees, elbows, and head.

The Rear "Crashing" Elbow utilizes forward movement and weight transference, coupled with a strong turning motion of the hips, to transfer force through the elbow into the target. This coupling of forward motion and hip turn is extremely powerful.

From the right rear punch, pull back the punching arm.

The punching arm should be pulled back using the hips—notice the change in position of the toes from the last photo. The right arm, shoulder, and hip should be pulled all the way back. The left shoulder and hip should be forward.

Launching yourself off the rear foot, take a step forward with your left foot. You must step at least the distance of the length of your forearm (this is because the last strike was a rear hand punch, which needs a longer reach), closing the distance to your attacker.

At the same time as you move forward, your hips should be turning—the left one pulling back, and the right one pushing forward—while you swing your elbow towards the target.

As you land, finish the turning motion of the hips to strike through the target with your elbow. Your other hand should remain up to guard your head, and possibly prepare to throw another elbow towards your assailant.

The targets for the Rear "Crashing" Elbow could be either the head/face, or if dealing with a much taller person, the xiphoid process located in the lower part of the sternum.

You want to connect with the tip of your elbow, and make sure that your chest is neither in front or behind, but rather level with the elbow. As with every strike, recoil your elbow after impact. Pull the hips back so they are now in a neutral position.

If your aggressor is significantly taller than you, and you don't believe they are wearing a suicide vest filled with explosives, you can attack the xiphoid process, a small piece of cartilage that hangs at the lower end of the sternum, as an alternative to the face.

Driving Knee

When delivering knee strikes, you need to make sure that power is transferred forward, rather than simply upwards. To have full power, a knee strike needs to have forward momentum to it, generated by a forward movement of the hips. Striking straight out with the knee, rather than upwards, also makes it a much more difficult strike to block.

Reach forward and take hold of your assailant, raising your knee straight up, but not towards them (if you raise it upwards towards your aggressor, they have a good chance of blocking it with their forearms), then push it straight out explosively, towards your assailant. This forward motion is extremely powerful and difficult to block. You should pull your opponent towards you as you do this.

Your knee strike now sets you up in a very strong position, from which you can execute a throw/takedown.

There are many ways to deliver knee strikes. One of the most powerful is to push the knee forward rather than upwards—this also makes the strike harder to block, e.g., when knee strikes are thrown in an upwards direction a block can be made against the large upper thigh muscle (quadriceps), but when the strike comes forward the only part available to perform a block against is the knee itself.

After throwing the rear crashing elbow, slide the rear foot in a little, in preparation for making a knee strike.

Start to bring the knee forward. You should visualize the hands coming up to grab on to and control your assailant. As well as striking them with your knee, you want to pull them onto it, combining both movements to generate power.

Raise the knee high. This is in preparation for driving it into your assailant. At this point, your knee should be facing the body part of your assailant you want to strike, e.g., lower ribs, sternum, face, etc. Your hips should be pulled back, ready to drive the knee forward.

Explosively drive your hips forward, pushing your knee into your assailant. At the same time pull back (with your hands), dragging them onto your knee.

Throws and Takedowns

Being able to put your assailant on the floor while you remain standing not only puts them in a very painful and disadvantaged position (hopefully unconscious or dazed), but it also makes a strong statement about who is controlling the fight. This is why the Krav Maga Yashir system contains a wide array of throws and takedowns—along with an extensive ground survival/fighting system.

After throwing the knee strike, step back with your right foot. You should still be holding on to your assailant.

Whenever you attempt to throw or take somebody down, you should use striking to put them in a disadvantageous position.

Take a step past the leg you are going to "reap"—in this example step past your assailant's right leg with your left (your left foot needs to be level with or beyond their right foot). Start to bring your right leg past theirs. You should be close to them, with little distance between you.

As you do this, catch their chin with your forearm, and tilt their head backwards. This movement should be used to direct all of their weight onto their supporting right leg, while at the same time taking them off balance.

While they are off balance, bring your right knee up high. All of their weight should be on their right leg—the one you are going to reap.

Forcefully swing your right leg backwards, catching the back of your assailant's knee with the back of yours. Your leg should swing like a pendulum and you should continue to lift your assailant's head, with your forearm, directing it towards the ground.

Continue to swing through with the leg, lifting the right leg of your assailant. You should aim to swing your right leg back as far and as high as you can. The more forceful the swing and the higher it goes, the harder the fall will be for your assailant.

Here is an alternate view, demonstrating the height of the reaping leg.

You should now push your attacker's head towards the ground. Do not follow them down. Your most advantageous position is to be standing while your assailant is on the ground. Here, you are able to deal with potential multiple assailants, and disengage from your assailant and the situation.

After you pull your assailant in for a knee strike, place your forearm under their chin. Before you put the foot of the leg making the knee strike back down, make a "scissor step" with your left leg, throwing your left foot forward as you bring your right leg back. You need your left foot to go at least level, and preferably further back, than your attacker's right leg.

Drive upwards (and back towards your attacker's right side) with your forearm to take their balance and load all of their weight onto their right leg; pull down on their right arm to help facilitate this. At the same time, bring your right knee upwards and behind your assailant.

Now swing your leg back, aiming to connect the back of your right knee with the back of their right knee. Do not put your foot down but continue to swing it upwards, lifting their leg as high as you can. This will direct their head towards the floor. Even if you haven't achieved a full knock-out, there will be a level of concussion and their body will have to recover from the effect of having exhaled all of the air from their lungs, a natural consequence of hitting the ground.

Conclusion

It is very rare that you will finish a fight with a single strike (even if it is a power strike), so although you should throw every strike with this intent, you should always throw your strikes in combinations, not stopping until your assailant is no longer able to engage in the confrontation. This can be achieved when they have emotionally crumbled and given up, are physically unable to continue (knocked out, broken limbs, etc.), or have removed themselves from the fight by running away. Alternatively, you can also look to your striking as something that creates opportunities for you to safely disengage from the conflict—but the situation you are in determines the solution.

It is worth remembering that the human body is capable of taking a lot of physical punishment, and because of this, delivering knock-out strikes is extremely difficult. Fortunately, most people will emotionally crumble and "give up" before their body does. By putting combinations of strikes together—that both deny your assailant the ability to make their own attack, as well as physically punish them and cause them pain—you will start to cause them to doubt their own ability, and this is the first step in getting them to emotionally crumble and give up the fight.

The Krav Maga Yashir Blocking System

If you have not been able to put yourself in a position to make a preemptive attack, you will, in all likelihood, find yourself having to defend against an assailant's strikes and punches (or even stabs, cuts, and slashes if they are armed with a knife). The following are descriptions of three methods for dealing with circular and straight attacks, whether they are with a weapon or empty-handed (punches/strikes).

Blocking Circular Strikes/360 Blocks

If somebody throws a circular punch (such as a haymaker), or even slashes at you with a knife, you will instinctively flinch, bringing your arm up to intercept whatever is coming towards you. It is important to note that you won't have time to distinguish the nature of the attack (whether it is a fist or a knife), rather you will simply react to the movement—you would make the same movement if you were walking across a park where a group is playing baseball, and the ball suddenly crosses your peripheral vision (your fear system will trigger this defense mechanism, regardless of the type of threat). We don't only look at the center of the chest (of our opponent) as a means of controlling range, but also as a way of allowing us to react naturally to strikes that cross our peripheral vision.

There are certain inherent movements that we make when facing an assault: We flinch when objects move quickly towards us and claw/grasp at anything that restricts our breathing. Krav Maga techniques are based on these natural responses. There are many things you might like to train yourself to do in a fight; however, it is almost impossible to retrain the hard-wired responses that the body naturally uses to defend itself. Krav Maga recognizes the way your body will respond when attacked, and works with these movements to create effective defenses.

When we detect a movement that enters our peripheral vision, we have a natural flinch response—this is something we don't have to train. Automatically, we will bring our arm inwards, to protect ourselves, and then push it out to meet the threat. We don't actually respond to the threat itself, but to the movement—it could be a punch, a knife attack, or even a child's ball.

In Krav Maga, when we defend circular strikes we use our flinch reflex as the starting movement—this is how we will react when a circular motion such as a punch, knife slash, or stab crosses into our peripheral vision. We can, of course, train our flinch response to be "better" by training it to contain a more forceful blocking action.

Rather than "passively" waiting for a strike, you should go to meet it by making an active defense, moving your arm towards the attack.

All blocking movements should be seen as attacks. Although protective, a block should also be seen as an assault on our assailant's arm. When you make such a block, you should look to drive your forearm into the attacking arm, with the aim of taking away any natural recoil it may have had while causing as much trauma to the limb as possible.

It is possible to improve instinctive movements and build on them. This is called creating an "assembly," using a natural reflex as the initial movement that starts off a set of trained/learned actions. Although the flinch reflex begins the defense, we want to train our block to be stronger and more effective than this reaction alone.

With the 360 Block, we want to ensure that the forearm is at a 90 degree angle to the upper arm, i.e., there is a 90 degree bend at the elbow. This angle ensures that the forearm will stop an attack as far away from the target as it can. This is in case the attack comes in the form of a swinging, stabbing attack, where the length of the full blade needs to be defended against rather than a slash, where you are likely dealing with just the last portion/end of the blade.

If someone attacks you with a downwards stabbing motion, e.g., an "Ice Pick"-style knife attack, you should raise your arm above your head forcefully to meet the strike. The angle of your arm at the elbow should be 90 degrees. You don't want to deflect the knife, but forcibly stop it—if the angle is greater than 90 degrees, the knife will slide down your arm, and possibly into your body. If the angle is less than 90 degrees then the knife will be too close to your head, and if it has a long blade your block may be ineffective. It is important to come and meet the knife arm, driving your forearm into it, and disrupting the timing of the recoil. Attackers usually recoil their knife in order to make multiple attacks.

If a person makes a slashing or circular stabbing motion towards your head, utilize your flinch reflex and bring your arm out to protect yourself. This same defense will work for a looping/circular punch as well. Again, maintain a 90 degree angle between the upper arm and forearm—in order to stop rather than deflect the strike.

It may be that a circular attack is aimed low rather than high. Such an attack might be a swinging/hooking punch to the kidneys, or a stabbing attack to the same target area.

Although pulling the arm into your side to "cover" the targeted areas works well when you are dealing with punches and kicks, it is not so effective against knives. Because we react to movement and not to the "nature" of the attack, our blocks are universal, used to defend against both armed and unarmed assaults.

If you are attacked in an upwards fashion—such as a knife shank/oriental style attack, drop your arm down and bend forward, pulling the hips back. Doing this is a natural body response when any movement towards the groin and lower body is detected—again, this is a movement you will make instinctively, and one that is almost impossible to overcome through training. Rather than try to work against the body's natural responses, Krav Maga aims to work with them.

This shows an **Upper 360 Block** to defend against a downward strike. This is not a particularly effective block against a stick/baton or bottle, since although you may block and stop the arm holding the weapon, the weapon has enough weight of its own to keep moving, and so in all likelihood will still strike you.

This shows a **Lateral 360 High Block** to defend against a punch being swung sideways at the head. This block would also work against a knife slash or stab towards the head.

This shows a **Lateral 360 Low Block** to defend against a punch or strike aimed at the kidneys or lower body. This block would also work against a knife slash or stab aimed at the same region.

This shows a **Downwards 360 Block** to stop a strike that is being swung upwards. In reality, such an attack is more likely to feature a knife being "shanked" upwards towards the groin and stomach, rather than a punch or hand strike.

This photo shows the importance of not having an angle of less than 90 degrees at the elbow. If your wrist is too close to your head when blocking circular strikes, an attacker stabbing with a knife may be able to stab you. With a 90 degree angle, you will have the full length of the upper arm to protect yourself from the length of the blade.

This photo shows the importance of coming out to meet the attacking arm. In this instance the block was passive, so the momentum of the assailant's arm has started to crush the block. Rather than waiting for an attack, the blocking arm should be pushed out, so that force meets force. This will prevent the block from folding inwards.

This photo shows the danger of having an angle of greater than 90 degrees at the elbow. If the arm is extended too far, it will deflect the knife to slide toward the defender's body. A block should stop the knife dead, not deflect it or give it movement.

The other thing to understand is that a block is meant to block, not deflect. This is especially important where edged weapons are concerned, as deflections give added movement to a knife, redirecting it in potentially unpredictable directions (one of the first tasks when dealing with knife attacks is to take away the movement of the weapon). This means the block has to stop the attack, meeting it head on. If the angle of the elbow is greater than 90 degrees, the knife could be deflected into the body.

Many people see "blocking" as defensive in nature. This is definitely the wrong mindset to have. In Krav Maga Yashir, every attack is met with an attack. When you use a 360 Block, you should be in the mindset that you are attempting to attack the arm that is punching, stabbing, or slashing at you—the idea is to cause an element of pain to the attacker in order to help disrupt the attack. If you can cause your assailant to associate every attack they make against you as causing them pain, they will begin to hesitate or stall before making an attack, and the more actions a person takes before making an assault slows it down and gives you more time to respond.

As well as educating the flinch response to end with a solid, attacking, 90 degree block, a body movement must be part of our defense. When you block a strike, step away from the attack, and towards your assailant.

A fundamental Krav Maga principle is "Hand Defense, Body Defense," i.e., any defense against an attack or threat must use these two components. Therefore, when we block with our hands/arms, we must also incorporate into this a body defense; i.e., we should move.

When making a 360 Block, you should accompany your hand defense (the blocking arm) with a movement away from the attack. It is important not to move away from your attacker, but towards them. You don't want to do this by simply moving directly forward, but by moving forward and to the side, positioning you offline.

When Imi Lichtenfeld first developed the original Krav Maga system, it was designed for infantry soldiers who carried packs on their backs. This meant that they had only one option when making a 360 Defense, and that was to move forward. Moving to the side with the weight of the pack on their back would have caused them to lose balance (also, they could use the weight of the pack to give them forward momentum).

As civilians unencumbered by such a constraint, we can move to the side as we move forward, putting us in a more advantageous position.

Your movement should position you so that you are facing your assailant at an angle, not head on. If they are throwing a circular strike, stab, or slash with their right hand, you should be moving away from the attack by stepping to the right, and towards your assailant's left shoulder, putting you in range to make your own attack.

You should always look to move to a stance/position from which you are able to launch your own attacks. If facing an aggressor at an angle rather than head on, your attacks are likely to be more successful, since your assailant will have to defend against them from their side, rather than from the front.

You should try to connect with your forearm as close to your assailant's wrist as possible. This will not only help you when you attempt to control their arm if it is a knife slash or stab, but will also give you a mechanical advantage from a leverage perspective, as the limbs are strongest closer to the body.

One of the dangers of stepping forward and into the attack, while making a simultaneous punch/strike, is that your movement and attack may cause your opponent to move backwards.

This may result in them dragging their knife across the blocking arm as they are moved backwards.

If you move in and to one side, your strike will move your opponent sideways, not backwards, and so the risk of getting cut is reduced—the knife is not likely to be dragged along your arm.

All Krav Maga techniques include both hand and body defense. We refer to this as a "200 percent defense"—should both the blocking arm and the body defense be 100% effective, the total defense will be 200% effective. All Krav Maga techniques have this redundancy built in—the hand defense should be enough on its own, as should the body defense. Combined, they should provide more than an adequate defense.

Every body movement you make should either set-up an attack or be part of the attack, and the 360 Block is no different. Rather than stepping away from the attacker, the body defense should take you towards them, moving you into an attacking position. Every defense should set up an attack—to not do this is to create and allow opportunities for your assailant to attack again.

The reason the 360 Block is so called is that it is used to defend against attacks from all circular angles, whether they be downwards or upwards (as in some knife attacks), or sideways, as with swinging punches and knife slashes.

If you have had the time to adopt an Interview Stance, your hands will be in front of your body, putting a defensive barrier between you and your attacker. This may force/limit them to making circular strikes. This is to your advantage, as they will have to break their shape to strike, giving you an additional alert of their attack. If you couple this with good relative body positioning and control of range, their attack will be relatively slow and cumbersome.

Simultaneous Blocking and Striking

One of the core principles of Krav Maga is that attack (unless preemptive) should be as close to defense as possible. This is so an attacker is limited to making just one strike/attack before having their assault immediately interrupted/disrupted by being attacked themselves. This is also an important emotional shift that a person being attacked must make—changing their mindset from defense into offense, and from that of victim to attacker. It is important to make the mental shift that puts you in the role of attacker, as your survival chances are increased by causing the maximum amount of pain, damage, injury, and harm to your assailant.

Just as we train the 360 Block to be an enhanced "flinch," we can also assemble a strike or punch to be combined with a blocking movement. If we make sure our 360 Forearm Block is actually an attack on the arm either punching or slashing at us, we will find that we naturally turn our hip into the block to add power to it. If we defend a right swinging punch with a left 360 Block, for example, we will have to turn our hips towards the attacking arm. This hip turn can be used to bring the right hip towards our attacker and throw either an eye strike, or if we are in a biomechanically strong position, a powerful punch. From this initial defense and attack, we can add the attacking sequence/combination described in the section on *Striking, Punching, Kicking and Throwing* (see pages 24–28). If you make a 360 Block with a simultaneous right punch, as in the example below, you could continue your counterattacking combination with a rear crashing elbow, a driving knee, and a Major Outer Reaping Throw.

Another fundamental Krav Maga principle is that defense should follow attack at the earliest opportunity. Rather than simply making a block, you should attempt to make some form of strike at the same time. You will never survive a real-life confrontation by simply blocking—you must at some point attack, and this should be at the earliest opportunity.

As you bring your arm up to block and move away from the strike, start to move your other arm (towards the target) in preparation for making a strike. Rather than punching, you may want to make an eye or throat strike that doesn't rely on having power to be effective. If you believe you can get in a strong enough position to do so, however, you should punch.

Your striking arm should start to extend out from your body. Make sure that you keep the elbow down, rather than splaying it out. You want to make sure that your punch has your body behind it, and if the elbow is positioned outwards this will not be the case.

As you make your strike/punch, your fist should be closing but not clenched. Clenching your fist prematurely will tense your arm and slow down your strike.

Time the clenching of your fist for when it makes impact with your assailant. Your arm should still have a degree of bend at the elbow at this point, as you will want to be able to extend/straighten it to drive through the target. Both feet should be planted on the floor at this time, so that you can drive off from them.

Start to extend the arm, and drive forcibly through the target. Your weight should be transferring to your forward leg in order to add body weight and real power to the strike.

Transfer your weight until around 60-70 percent of it is on the forward foot, while at the same time continuing to extend the arm, and drive through the target. At this point you should either disengage completely, disengage to get an improvised weapon (or draw your own), or continue to strike and/or control your aggressor.

When you throw a punch or make a strike, you need to be aware of the consequences of your actions. If you punch somebody, they are likely to move backwards. If the assailant tries a circular stab and you block and punch but stay in front of them, they are likely to move back as a consequence of the strike, dragging the knife across your arm. If you move away from the knife and towards their opposite shoulder—with your normal body defense—you will be punching them from an angle, which will move them not directly backwards, but off to the side.

Defending Straight Punches and Strikes

If you have the time to adopt an Interview Stance, and can put up your hands up in front of you, you will severely limit your attacker's ability to make straight strikes. Preventing your assailant from making straight strikes that are both fast and don't require their shape to change/break forces them to make circular strikes to attack you, which are easier to identify and block. If you are not able to prevent your attacker from making straight strikes and punches, you must at least control the range, so you force them to move their body before, or during, the strike. This will provide you with a larger movement to respond to.

Pat Away Defenses

A straight punch will always contain recoil. That is, nobody will punch and leave the arm hanging in space without drawing it back. It should also be noted that punches are thrown in combinations, rather than singularly. This means that the body defense that accompanies the hand defense has to take both of these things into account, and should result in you moving offline. Even if you are able to block the first punch thrown, if you don't move you will be a sitting duck for the one that follows.

The "Pat Away Defense" simply involves a palm strike/slap to the forearm to move the strike to the side, while the body defense moves you away from the strike and towards your attacker. Your blocking hand should mirror your attacker's punching hand—if the attacker throws a right punch, your left hand should intercept it and you should move to your left, and vice versa. This will move you away from the attacker's other "live" hand, which, if they are punching in combinations, you will want to avoid (we refer to this as moving to the "dead side," e.g., away from the other live hand, which could be used to attack you).

With the Pat Away Defense, you do not wait to receive the strike, but will look to intercept it at the earliest opportunity—ideally at the very moment it is thrown. Moving your hand to meet the strike as soon as you can will help you close it down before it gains momentum and speed (rather than in its later stages, when it is moving faster). If you can control the range to make your assailant step or move as part of the attack, this body movement will telegraph the punch and give you a clear signal that a strike is being thrown.

As soon as you see someone go to make a straight strike/punch, move your hand towards it in a striking motion. You should think of your palm making an attack on the punching arm, deflecting it forcibly away from its intended target. Use the hand that mirrors the punch to block it, e.g., if it is a right punch, your left hand should make the block.

At the same time as you make the block, make a step to the same side, and towards your assailant—if you block with the left hand, move to your left. Your right hand should start to move towards your attacker's punching shoulder.

By moving the arm across your attacker's body you will prevent them from striking with their other arm.

Your block should land with enough force that is causes the attacker to turn their torso and present you with their shoulder. By moving the punching arm away so forcefully, you will have also created the space to move toward their shoulder easily.

Grab your assailant's clothing around the shoulder area tightly. Do not worry if their t-shirt seems flimsy and weak. If you know the directions where all types of clothing are strong, you can use an aggressor's clothing against them. It is possible to perform very dramatic throws using a person's t-shirt—if you know where to take hold.

You can use your assailant's clothing to control their movement by pulling them towards you for knee strikes, throws, and takedowns, for example.

If from this position your opponent tries to turn towards you to make another attack...

...They will find their throat/windpipe pushed against your forearm, and in a position where you can control their head, and therefore their movement.

This photo shows the importance of using the hand directly facing the punching arm to block with—if you block a left punch with your left arm, as in the example, you will allow your attacker the freedom to make a punch with their right hand. At the same time, you will have no free hand to block with.

This photo shows the importance of blocking across rather than patting the punch down. If you pat the punch down you give your assailant the space (a "channel") to make a strike with their other hand. Your block should aim to jam up your attacker's other hand by deflecting the punch into it.

The hand that pats the strike away should not pat the strike downwards, but rather across the attacker's body. If the punching arm is moved downwards, it clears space and makes room for the other hand to strike. If it is patted away across the attacker's body, then it has the potential to get in the way of the other hand and jam up your assailant.

Gaining Control of Your Attacker

In many cases, it is good to grab your assailant's shoulder or clothing, in order to control their movement. This will help limit their ability to throw other attacks, and allow you to throw your own. If you block a right punch with your left hand and move to your left (your attacker's right side), you should grab their right shoulder with your right arm—if you tuck your chin down, your grabbing arm can be used to protect your head against a strike from your attacker's other hand.

As you move forward you should also pull your assailant's shoulder towards you, as this will help upset their balance (if you have forced them to move and commit their body forward as part of their strike, their weight will be heading in this direction anyway, so you will be working with their momentum).

If, while you have control of the shoulder, your assailant should turn to make another attack, they will find that your forearm is against their windpipe. If you react to their movement by thrusting your forearm into their throat, you will compromise their balance, while putting yourself in a strong position to attack with knees, or execute a throw/takedown.

Inner Forearm Blocks

The Inner Forearm Block has many uses. It can be an effective defense against a straight knife stab (which is not the most common street attack with a knife), as well as straight strikes against the body. It is especially useful as a defense when an attacker is striking at a close range, or they are striking within your arm's length, and where a last-minute defense to protect yourself is necessary.

The key to the Inner Forearm Block is to let the elbow lead the arm movement, rather than the wrist or hand. The reason for this is to force the body to follow the movement, turning as the elbow moves—this is facilitated by turning on the ball of the same side foot. (If you are using your left forearm to block, you will need to pivot on the ball of your left foot, pulling your right shoulder back). The idea is to not only intercept the strike with your forearm, but to turn your body sideways to allow the attack to go past you.

In almost all instances, the body should move the hands and arms rather than the other way round. Blocking using the inner forearm is no exception—the torso should turn, moving the forearm to meet the punch/strike.

Rather than thinking about making contact with the wrist, there should be an emphasis on bringing the elbow upwards using the turning motion of the body. This will ensure that the body turns, allowing the attack to pass by it. This is the "body defense" component of the block.

As you feel your forearm make contact with the attacker's arm, start to rotate your arm, turning your hand in to face you. This rotation will assist in "pulling" the attacker's arm forward and past you, and forcing them to commit weight forward, which will effect their subsequent mobility.

Your finishing position should see your assailant almost pass by you and leave you "bladed" to the side of them. A quick shift in weight will allow you to turn and close range with your attacker. This will position you away from your assailant's other hand.

This same defense works well against a straight knife stab (these are fairly uncommon attacks from a civilian perspective). When dealing with a knife, rotating your arm to assist in "pulling" the attacker's arm forward becomes all the more important, as one of your goals when dealing with weapons is to get yourself behind them. Therefore you want the weapon as far past you as possible.

The Inner Forearm Block is a good defense against a push (especially if the push is to be followed by a punch), as by turning the body sideways, otherwise known as "blading," you prevent your assailant from being able to push against your chest or upper body. The forearm block becomes useful in such an assault, because a person needs to be closer to you than with a punch—as they need to be able to generate power to move you. This means they are probably too close to you for a pat away defense to be used.

Conclusion

A fight or violent confrontation should be defined by you launching a continuous assault upon your aggressor. By working preemptively and with full aggression, you should aim to prevent your assailant from pulling a weapon or catching you in any hold or control—obviously this is not always possible, so you need to know how to deal with these attacks, as well.

PART 2

Self-Defense Scenarios

Armed Assaults

Different Types of Armed Assault

A person shows you they have a weapon for a reason. They may be showing it to you to convince you to hand over your wallet, or to make you move with them to another location. It could be that they don't intend to use the weapon but merely want to intimidate you, either to force you to comply with a demand or to scare you so that you back away. It may be that they intend to use the weapon against you, but aren't yet emotionally ready to do so—they may need to build themselves up first by feeding off your fear. If they're emotionally ready, and intend to assault you, you'll likely never see the weapon before it is actually used.

This section looks at armed assaults, both as threats and as attacks. There is a big difference between attacks and threats as far as the assailant's intent to use the weapon is concerned. If an assailant attacks you with a knife, it is clear that they are intending to cause you harm. If someone threatens you with a weapon (stating or implying that if you don't comply with their demands they will use it), their intent is not so clear. It could be that if you hand over your wallet, purse, cell phone, etc. to an armed mugger, they will let you go unharmed.

The Similarities between Gun and Knife Controls/Disarms

Krav Maga Yashir is a system founded on concepts and principles. This means that techniques based on common and shared principles will have a tendency to look the same and replicate each other. In a weapon threat, the positioning of the weapon, the relative body positioning of the assailant, and the target are often more important than the type of weapon used—whether it is a knife or a gun.

All of our weapon controls and disarms adhere to these basic principles:

1. There must be a body defense as well as a hand defense.
2. Two hands must be used to control the weapon arm.
3. Your body must be positioned behind the weapon.
4. All disarms and controls must be powered by the body.
5. The weapon must always be used against the assailant.

If you can get two hands on the weapon arm to control both your assailant and the weapon, while staying behind the weapon, you will be safe from that threat. If your control can take away or restrict the movement of the weapon, you will prevent your assailant from continuing to use it. These rules apply equally to a knife as they do a gun.

Because of the similarities between the different weapon controls and disarms, defenses against gun and knife threats are shown alongside each other in this section of the book.

Knife Disarming

You should only disarm somebody of a knife for one reason: To use it against them or others in your environment (as with multiple assailants). Simply disarming somebody of a weapon doesn't prevent them from attacking you again, nor does it mean they won't use another weapon they have on their person against you. If you can use your assailant's own weapon against them while they are still holding it, you will have prevented them from making any further assault, while keeping your fingerprints off the blade. Knife disarming is taught at higher levels in our system, along with how to properly use the knife offensively.

Financial Predators

Most people hold to "Models of Violence" which suggest that the majority of muggings and street robberies take place in back alleys and other deserted places. The truth is that muggers, just like other predators, will go where their prey is—this means that most muggings take place in crowded areas, where there is a ready supply of cash-rich victims. A mugger will use crowds to disguise their synchronization of movement to their intended target.

For an assailant to assault you, they must first tie their movement to yours. They may do this by directly approaching you, following you, waiting for you at a particular location (such as your house or car), or intercepting you en route (for example, they could walk at an angle alongside you to cut you off as you head to your car).

One way in which we can increase our situational awareness is to learn to identify when people adjust their movements based on ours. For an assailant to attack us they first have to get close to us. If we can identify the different ways they can synchronize their movements to us, we have a chance to identify a threat before we experience it.

Rather than make a direct approach to their intended victim, the aggressor sets a course that will see them cross paths at some point. In many instances, this could be a natural stopping point, such as a road that must be crossed—which will force their victim to slow down or stop—or another location that facilitates their assault.

It can be difficult to identify when somebody is trying to intercept us, because they will generally close distance slowly, and at an angle where it is difficult for us to determine if they are trying to get close to us, or are simply heading in the same direction. If you believe somebody has synchronized their movement to yours, you can always change direction, and see if they do the same.

A busy street, shopping mall, or transit station on a Saturday afternoon provides a mugger with a steady supply of potential victims, and good cover for approaching whoever they have targeted, without their movement being picked up. The fact that most people feel safe from violence when in populated areas means that whoever they select is likely to be extremely surprised when they are assaulted. The more surprised a person is, the more likely they are to comply with any demand made of them, especially if a weapon is present.

An assailant can synchronize their movement to yours by directly approaching you. This type of synchronization may seem easy to identify. However, if an assailant uses a crowd to disguise their movement, it may be difficult to spot what they are doing. Many muggings happen in relatively busy areas, where bystanders are used to block and obscure what is going on.

An attacker can also follow you. We are usually very good at picking up on this type of synchronization, with our adrenal/fear system alerting us to the sound of footsteps behind us. Unfortunately, many people deny what is happening and reassure themselves by explaining away misgivings, presuming that the person behind them is probably harmless, and reasoning that they are overreacting.

If an assailant knows where you are heading, they can get there before you and wait. Using your car's remote key fob to locate it in a parking lot can alert any potential attacker to where you are heading (it also opens your car—the one safe place you have in the environment), enabling them to get there in advance and wait for you.

Should you suddenly find yourself the target of a mugging, your first thought should always be to comply—it is never worth risking your life for possessions. However, if after complying with a demand your assailant doesn't leave, then you know that there is something else they are after (probably you), and you will need to engage with them physically.

Victim Facilitators

Just as there are things that your assailant does before making an assault, there are behaviors and actions that you may well do, that will identify you as a potential victim, such as appearing unaware of your environment, moving in a way that is out of synch with your surroundings, etc. If you walk with your eyes to the ground you will not only appear unobservant, but may convey an image of sadness, depression, and low self-esteem. This body language will tell a predator that you are unlikely to fight back and will likely be more willing to acquiesce to their demands.

Knife Low to Front

In most mugging situations where other people are present the weapon will remain low and hidden from passersby. The criminal's greatest fear is getting caught, so they will be surreptitious with their threat.

If you have failed to spot a mugger who has synchronized their movement to yours, you may find yourself having to deal with a knife pressed into your stomach. Your first response should be to hand over your wallet. However, if they then don't leave the scene, you should be prepared to deal with them physically. First, you need to raise your hands level with the knife.

With an underhand grip, explosively grab the wrist of the hand holding the knife and push it towards the attacker, jamming it up against them—your first task when dealing with a weapon is to restrict its movement. At the same time, pull your body back—if the knife has actually been pressed into you, possibly even puncturing your flesh, this will help clear it, without you getting cut (or further cut).

Immediately bring your second hand to grip over the hand holding the knife—this will prevent your attacker from passing the knife to their free hand. With both hands/arms in this position, if your attacker tries to push the knife back towards you, they will simply end up driving your elbows into your stomach, rather than the knife.

Once you have restricted the movement of the knife, and have two hands on the arm holding the knife (one on the wrist and one over the hand), start to drive your assailant backwards. Whoever controls the movement of the fight, controls the fight. You want your assailant to start thinking about staying balanced and on their feet, rather than about the knife.

Because you are going to use your assailant's knife against them, you need to create some space in order for the knife to move. With both hands, "punch" into your attacker's stomach, and pull the knife arm back. This should all be done while you are pushing them and they are concentrating on their footwork and movement, rather than on retaining/using the weapon.

Once you have created the space to use the knife, slash it across your assailant's side, dragging the knife forcibly across their body. Rather than simply using arm strength to make this slashing movement, step past them, slashing their side with the knife as you do so. Most people react to knife slashes as if they've received an electric shock and will pull their body away.

You should now find yourself at your aggressor's side, with the knife pointed towards them.

Slide your left arm (the one that was grabbing the attacker's wrist), under the elbow of the attacker's knife arm. At the same time, you should move to face them and pull the hand holding the knife towards your hips. Your attacker's forearm should be pressed firmly against your body, with their knife pointed towards the side of their body.

Explosively drive upwards with the hips, pushing the knife into them. At no point should your fingerprints be on the knife, as your right hand should still be wrapped around the attacker's hand, which is holding it.

Every physical solution you take should comprise of a hand defense and a body defense (this is a fundamental Krav Maga principle). Your hand defense in this situation will be to grab your assailant's wrist using an underhand grip, and push the knife directly into your attacker's stomach, while your body defense will see you pull your hips directly back. If your assailant has already pushed the knife into you (and many assailants will do this to show that they are serious about the threat, and to limit your defensive options), moving your body back will mean you won't cut yourself when you make your hand defense.

As soon as you can, get your other hand around the attacker's knife hand (as well as adding to control, this will also stop your aggressor from passing the knife to their free hand). You should use the same underhand grip to do this. Using underhand grips, as opposed to overhand ones, will bring your elbows into your body, and make it mechanically impossible for your aggressor to push the knife back into you. The knife should be pressed firmly against your assailant's body, restricting its movement to prevent its further use, and giving your attacker problems of their own to deal with.

Start to move your aggressor so that their focus is on maintaining balance, rather than on retaining or using the knife. Once you have them moving, make a punching motion into your attacker's stomach with both hands, to make room for you to move the knife.

Turn the wrist of the attacker's knife hand to direct the blade at their midriff, while at the same time stepping out to the side. This will allow you to use their own knife to slash them.

Now turn to face their side, slipping your left arm through to secure your assailant's forearm against your body. The knife should now be at your hips, pointing towards your attacker. Explode with your hips, driving the knife into their body.

Gun to Front of Body

Dealing with a gun threat low to the front is almost identical to dealing with a knife. The same initial hand and body defense is made—the hips are pulled back in this instance to free any clothing that may get caught and trap the barrel, keeping it pointed at you, as you make your hand defense.

This time, instead of grabbing the hand that is holding the knife, you should grab the barrel of the gun, using an underhand grip. Not only will this allow you to get your elbows pressed into your body, but it will prevent you from muzzling your own hand with the gun—something which is hard to avoid with an overhand grip.

As with the knife defense, push into your attacker to move them and focus their concern on their balance. As they move backwards, make a rapid punching motion into their stomach while holding on to the gun, to create the space necessary to perform the disarm.

Once you have room, turn your hips and step in. Hold the weapon arm at the wrist with your left hand, and, with your right hand still on the barrel of the gun, punch rapidly through the space between your assailant's arm and body. This should rip the weapon from their grip. Immediately use the gun to strike at the face of your assailant.

Although it may be tempting to think about disengaging and using the weapon as a firearm, the truth is that you know nothing about this weapon (whether it is loaded, whether it became jammed during disarming, or even if it was ever operable). What you do know is that it is a good, solid object that can be used as an impact weapon.

Disarming a gun is very similar to controlling a knife from this position (all of the controls/disarms in Krav Maga Yashir work for any type of weapon). When you raise your hands to be level with the gun, shrug and look frightened. You want your assailant to believe they are in control, and don't have to worry about you as a threat.

With an underhand grip, explosively push the attacker's weapon hand (and weapon) into their stomach. Make sure that you don't push the barrel across your other hand. Make a body defense by pulling the body directly back, to make sure the barrel of the gun doesn't get caught up in any loose clothing.

You should end up in a position where your free hand is pulled out of the way of the gun and your body "bladed," i.e., turned to the side. You can lean into your assailant—with your elbow tucked inwards—to help restrict the movement of the weapon by applying your body weight against the weapon hand.

Immediately get your second hand to the weapon, grabbing the barrel in an underhand grip. An overhand grip on the gun would result in you "muzzling" your own hand and would be virtually impossible against a snubnosed revolver or pistol.

Immediately start to drive your attacker backwards, controlling their movement. They should be thinking more about how to move their feet and stay upright, than about using the weapon.

At this point you have control of the weapon, and your assailant, but you have not disarmed your assailant. While you drive them backwards, punch the gun into their stomach, and then pull back on the weapon arm. This will create the space you need to perform the disarm.

With the hand that is holding the firearm "punch" your arm through as you pull back on your assailant's wrist. The majority of the force will come from the punching arm holding the gun. You should aim to generate the same amount of power you would with a closed fist punch.

Before disengaging, strike your assailant with the weapon. Do not rely on it being an operational firearm—it could be jammed, unloaded, or even an imitation or replica pistol/gun. Also, shooting someone might not immediately stop them from fighting back, if they are highly adrenalized, whereas knocking them unconscious with a solid lump of metal will.

Knife to Rear of Body (Low)

It is always worth considering an individual's reason for being in a location. Someone waiting by an ATM for an extended period of time is something to question. (Few predators will be so obvious and will instead choose locations such as parking lots, transit stops, and shopping malls, where they have a chance to blend in with other commuters, shoppers, or travelers.)

If a mugger is waiting for you in a particular location, they need to make themselves appear "legitimate," as if they have a good reason to be in the environment. A mugger who is approaching you as part of a crowd of shoppers has legitimacy and can use the crowd to disguise their movements. However, if they are coming towards you wearing street clothes, while the other commuters in the group are wearing business dress, they may appear out of place, or more noticeable. If a person is standing next to an ATM but shows no intention of using it, they are out of place. However, if the same person stands behind you as if they are waiting to use the machine, they now appear legitimate in the setting.

Any assailant on the street will try to deny you the time to react and the distance needed to physically defend yourself. In reality, things will happen faster and in less space than you are probably used to in a training environment.

An assailant lurking at an ATM is likely to wait until you have withdrawn your money before attempting to mug you. If you feel that the person behind you is too close, not giving you enough room, and is generally acting inappropriately for that setting, just announce in an exasperated voice that your company hasn't deposited your wages again, and leave without making a withdrawal. You should always be extra aware of what is going on behind you, especially during the time that the machine can be heard counting out the money—this is a clear signal to any predator that your transaction is complete and a good time for them to make their advance and put a weapon to your back.

A mugger/financial predator may not approach you from the front, but instead come from the rear. While we are withdrawing money from an ATM we are vulnerable to such threats. The assailant will likely give his victim some space so that they feel comfortable making a withdrawal, and only moved up behind when the money is being counted move up behind.

If you find yourself with a weapon at your back, your first task is to ascertain which hand is holding the weapon. It could be that the mugger is actually putting their finger in your back, prodding you, while they hold the weapon in their other hand. Through clothing it is not always easy to tell the difference between a knife/gun and a finger.

Look over both shoulders to check if you can see which of your assailant's hands is holding the weapon, and which is empty. You won't be able to see the weapon itself, but if you can see that the left hand is empty, you can deduce that the right hand is holding the weapon.

Keeping both hands low, and the arm closest to the knife arm straight, pivot on the toes of the opposite foot to turn, using your arm to move the knife away from your body, while at the same time pulling your body away from the knife; employing both a hand defense and a body defense.

Your first task is to take away the movement of the weapon. A knife has to have room to move in order to cut, slash, or stab. By pressing your attacker's knife arm against their body with your forearm, you restrict their ability to move and use the knife against you. To increase the pressure on the attacker's knife arm, you can lean in to them somewhat.

As you turn and your arm starts to make contact with your assailant's knife arm, your other hand should chase round with an underhand grip to grab your assailant's wrist. You should be grabbing the wrist at almost the same time as your other arm makes contact with the assailant's weapon arm.

Complete your turn so you are now facing your assailant. You should now slide the arm up that was pressing against your assailant's weapon arm, so that you can make an underhand grip over the hand that is holding the weapon—this prevents them passing their knife to their free hand.

In reality, few assailants think about moving the weapon from one hand to the other. Most armed assailants are so single-minded that if they are holding a knife with their right hand, they will continue to hold it this way even if it makes more sense to change it to their left. It is, however, better to deny them such an opportunity.

Start to push into the assailant, driving them backwards and pushing the knife into them.

When you are ready to use their knife against them, and they are concentrating more on their footwork than on attacking you, punch the knife into their stomach and then pull their knife arm back. You should have now created enough space to slash/cut them with their knife.

Without changing grip, step past them, dragging the knife across the side of their body.

Working this way is easier than trying to disarm them, as you are not having to fight against somebody who wants to hold on to their weapon. In fact, you want them to keep hold of their weapon.

In this photo, you can see how it is the body, rather than the arm, which powers the cutting motion. Using your whole body against the strength of one limb makes it possible to perform this technique against much stronger and more powerful individuals.

After you have slashed the attacker and stepped passed them, start to turn to face them, in preparation for using the knife in a more conclusive way.

Thread your left arm under their elbow, while bringing the knife hand towards your hips. (At no point should your fingerprints be on the knife.)

Thread your arm fully through, so your elbow is positioned on/below your assailant's elbow. If you are sweaty or feel that you need to secure the arm further, you can grab your own shirt with your free hand. This makes it virtually impossible for your attacker to release their arm.

Using your hips, drive upwards, forcing the assailant's knife into their side. Keep the hand that is holding their hand pinned to your hips, so you are using body rather than arm strength to power this movement.

Before making a defense, you should ascertain which hand is holding the weapon. Look over both shoulders and try to see, firstly, which hand is holding the knife or gun; and secondly, whether it is the knife or gun that is being held to your back, or if your assailant instead has their hand pressed to you, with the weapon held back. If, when you look behind you, you see an empty hand, you know that it is the knife that is against you. If you see the knife being held back, you know it is the assailant's hand which is pressing into you. In the following scenario, we will assume it is the knife that is held directly against your back.

First, shrug your shoulders to bring your wrists level with the weapon hand. (When you turn, you want to connect wrist-to-wrist with your assailant.) You can make this look like a submissive and scared gesture, so as to not alert your assailant to your impending defense.

To initiate both a hand and a body defense, pivot on the ball of your left foot to bring your right arm around to connect with the wrist of your assailant's knife hand. Your other hand chases this movement to seize your attacker's wrist, using an underhand grip.

Step into your assailant with your right leg, and use your right arm to push their knife arm against their body (you should now be facing them). This will take the chance of any further movement of the knife away—and for a knife to be usable, it must have room to move.

Now transition your right hand to take control of the attacker's hand that is holding the knife, also using an underhand grip, and start to push them backwards. As you do this, make a punching motion to their stomach to create space in which to move the knife.

Now step out with your left foot, dragging the knife across the assailant's midriff, and turn to the side, slipping your left arm to secure their forearm against your body. The knife should now be at your hips, pointing towards your attacker. Explode from your hips, driving the knife into their body.

Gun to Rear of Body (Low)

Your initial movement to turn and push the weapon arm into your attacker is identical to that of "knife control" from this position. However, rather than transitioning your right hand to your assailant's weapon hand, you move it to take control of the barrel of the gun, in a similar underhand grip to that of your left hand.

Now, push the gun into your assailant's stomach and start to push them backwards and make a punching motion to their stomach to create space to move the gun.

Holding the left wrist firmly, use the leverage advantage offered by the barrel of the gun to bend the wrist and punch strongly through, while pulling back with the left hand to release the gun. Use the gun to repeatedly strike your assailant before disengaging.

Always be aware of those who show an unusual interest in you. Simply being aware of who is in your environment, and letting them know you are aware of them, is often enough to avoid becoming the victim of a violent crime. Assailants want to deny you time and distance in which to react, and demonstrating you are aware of their presence can prevent this.

Here, instead of a knife, the mugger places a gun at your back. If they want money (which, considering the situation, is their most likely demand), you should acquiesce and give it to them. Only if they don't then leave should you consider a physical solution.

Rather than putting your hands straight up in the air, which would take them a long way from the weapon, shrug your shoulders upwards to bring your hands/wrists level with your assailant's weapon. As when dealing with the knife from behind, you should glance behind you to ascertain which hand is holding the weapon.

Turn your body and use the nearest arm to move the firearm out of the way—your turn should also pull your body out of the line of fire. Now reach your other hand round in an underhand grip to take control of the wrist of the assailant's weapon arm.

The hand of the arm that turned the gun away should now be used to grab the gun in an underhand grip.

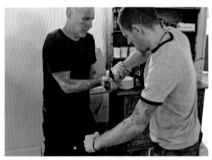

Begin to turn the gun inwards towards the assailant, and away from yourself. This will also weaken the assailant's grip. You should think of using the length of the barrel like a lever to turn the gun away from yourself and toward the assailant.

Now explosively "punch" through with the gun while pulling back on the wrist.

Your punch should have as much force as a regular strike, and should literally rip the gun out of your assailant's hand.

Without changing your grip on the gun, use it as an impact weapon against your assailant before disengaging.

Knife to Side of Body (Low)

An assailant may not approach you directly from behind, but may make their approach to your side. It might be that they follow you back to your car after using an ATM and wait until you are distracted by opening your car door before putting their knife directly to your side and making a demand for your money. This is a good use of the environment on their part, as they can use the open car door to hide their assault from passersby.

Your hand defense will involve grabbing the wrist of the knife hand with your nearest hand, while your body defense will see you pulling your body directly back, away from the knife. This is particularly important when the knife has been pushed into you.

Once again, push the knife into your assailant's stomach, to restrict its movement and further use.

You should now take a large step back and towards your aggressor, moving to the outside of their arm to get behind the weapon. Your furthest hand should follow your body movement and get an underhand grip on the hand of your assailant that is holding the knife.

Now turn, bending the wrist, and drag the knife across your assailant's midriff.

Once done, step once more with your left foot past your assailant's shoulder, securing their weapon arm with your left arm, and bring their knife hand to your hip. Use your body to thrust the knife upwards into their side.

An assailant may approach you from the side. This might be due to a certain activity you are engaging in, such as getting into a car, or turning away from an ATM, which presents your side to a would-be attacker. As naturally as you can you should move your hands into a position where they can quickly control and re-direct the weapon/weapon hand, should you need to.

With an underhand grip, grab the attacker's wrist, while at the same time pulling your body away from the knife.

As you take a step backwards and towards your assailant, pull the knife past you. This movement should literally pull the assailant's knife hand towards your other hand, and should get you behind the weapon.

With your other hand, clasp the knife hand of the assailant. This will prevent them from passing the knife to their free hand. Both of your hands should have an underhand grip, so that it is mechanically impossible for your assailant to move the knife back to its original position.

Immediately turn the knife towards your attacker and start to move past them, cutting/slashing their side with the knife.

Continue moving past them. One reason for constantly moving, realigning, and changing position is that you force your aggressor to keep processing new information, and so make it hard for them to work out how to keep attacking you.

Once you have moved from being in front of your attacker to their side, use your arm that was holding the wrist to thread through and control your assailant's forearm.

This photo shows the arm being threaded through from the opposite side.

Once the arm has been completely threaded through to the point where both elbows meet, and the hand controlling the knife hand has been pulled to the hips, drive upwards and towards your attacker, stabbing them with their own knife.

Gun to Side of Body (Low)

If the weapon is a gun rather than a knife, you can make an almost identical defense.

Instead of grabbing the hand that holds the weapon, your furthest hand should follow your body and get an underhand grip on the barrel of the gun. Make sure that the hand stays close to the body when you move, so the gun doesn't muzzle your right hand. In this situation you don't need to push the gun into your attacker's body, but simply bring it to their side.

Now turn with your body, so that your hips are facing your assailant. This will bend their wrist, and bring the barrel of the gun around to point at them.

Hold the attacker's wrist firmly with your left hand, then pull back, while at the same time punching forward with your right hand to perform the disarm. You can now use the gun as an impact weapon to strike at your assailant repeatedly, before disengaging.

We are watched and analyzed far more times than we actually realize. We may think that our actions and behaviors are insignificant to those around us—however, we should understand how they may help facilitate a crime. Withdrawing money from an ATM while someone not intending to use it is present sends us a clear signal that we lack awareness, thus identifying us as an easy target.

Before someone uses a weapon, they have to first draw it—few people walk around with a weapon in full view (you should train from the perspective of an assailant drawing a weapon, as well as having it already drawn). If you are alert/aware, and can spot this movement as it is happening, you should "spoil the draw" and prevent the weapon from being used in the first place.

When a firearm is presented to you from side-on, get your hands level with the weapon as soon as possible. As long as you can present an image of yourself as a scared individual who will do whatever your assailant wants, they are unlikely to question the exact position of your hands.

Grab your assailant's wrist and pull the gun past you. Take a step towards your attacker, so you are also moving past the gun.

With the hand grabbing the assailant's weapon arm, "feed" the gun to your other hand. Your other hand should grab the weapon with an underhand grip. Make sure that you have a good grip, because if the gun is a semi-automatic and it fires, your grip could prevent the slide moving back, and so jam the weapon.

Turn and "punch" through once you have a good grip on the gun, making sure you pull back on the wrist at the same time.

There are few more powerful body movements than punching—if you can try to visualize all movements as striking ones, you will find that you add power and speed to everything you do.

Once you have disarmed the assailant of their gun, immediately start to use their firearm as an impact weapon, delivering the maximum concussive force as possible. Never rely on the gun being operational as a firearm, and understand that unless you can shoot a hip or a joint to "mechanically" disable their movement, they may be able to keep attacking—even with a bullet in them.

Sticking to the Script

When dealing with muggers and other predatory individuals, it is important to stay "on script," and not add any new ideas into the situation. Avoid saying things like "Don't kill me," or "I'll do anything you want." A mugger may have the primary motive of robbing you, but they may also have secondary motives, such as raping you. Saying things like, "I'll do anything you want" may convince them that they will be able to get away with this more serious assault, too. In the situation where the mugging occurs near your car, you may have initially mistaken the mugger for a car thief. If you'd responded to their threats with, "Take the car, please, just don't hurt me," you may well have introduced the idea of taking the car, in addition to their planned assault.

Muggings and Street Robberies where the Assailant Uses the Environment

Knife Threat Against a Wall

Just as you should look to use the environment to your own advantage (using objects as barriers, weapons, and shields, for example), your assailant may also use the environment to their advantage, pinning you against walls, doors, etc., to restrict your movement—while at the same time increasing the overall sense of the danger you are in.

If you are in the lobby of an ATM, your assailant may force you back against a wall and stick a knife to your throat. In this setting, they don't have to be so concerned with keeping their weapon out of sight, as being inside the lobby offers them some protection in this regard.

Although it may seem counter-intuitive, you should press your neck/throat towards the knife, so that you can maintain some space between your head and the wall—this is so that when you make your defense, you can pull your throat back, away from the knife. Do not worry too much about getting cut—knives are designed to slice and stab, not to press. (In certain situations, it is possible to make a knife disarm by pressing down with your hand on the blade itself.)

As you lean in, bring your open hands up to the height of your attacker's wrist, "crying them into position," with your palms facing towards the attacker's arm. This is an expected movement and one that your aggressor will be more surprised if you don't make—your assailant will expect you to bring your hands up in a submissive fashion when they present a weapon.

With your hands in this position, explosively pull down on their weapon arm, with your right hand on their forearm near the elbow and your left hand on their wrist. Pull their arm and lock it into your body to gain a better control and take away any further movement of the knife.

As you do this, make a small body defense by pulling your head back away from the knife, into the space you created when you pressed your throat towards it.

Now turn your body to the right, pivoting on the ball of your left foot. This will start you moving away from the wall. At the same time, pull your assailant's elbow with your right hand to straighten it against your body, while bringing your left arm over so that you have the arm locked under your armpit. From here, you can start to use the environment against your assailant by repeatedly slamming their head into the wall.

Now change the underhand grip of your right hand to an overhand grip and join your left hand to your right wrist, making a "figure four" lock.

Make a strong pulling motion to extend the arm, taking your aggressor's balance, and then explosively push the knife towards their throat in a circular fashion. After cutting their throat (while they are still holding the knife), you can take them to ground and either continue stabbing them, or if they are no longer a threat, disengage.

Be aware that as soon as you go to control or disarm a weapon you will be forcing your assailant to use it, turning a threat scenario into an attacking one. A mugger's script may have them not intending to use their weapon should you comply with their demands, but as soon as you try to control their weapon they will attempt to retain it, and then use it against you. In such a situation, you must also be prepared to use the weapon against them—to not think this way would be to hand a tactical advantage to your assailant.

Assailants may well use the environment to assist them in their crimes. A wall can be used to restrict movement and make a victim feel that their options are limited. If an assailant puts a knife to our throat and pushes us up against a wall, we will probably feel trapped, with little option but to acquiesce to their demands.

As counter-intuitive as it may seem, when someone holds a knife to your throat, you should press yourself into it, rather than allow your head to be pushed fully back against the wall. Having this space behind your head allows you to move your throat back away from the knife, so that you can explosively pull down on the weapon arm with both hands.

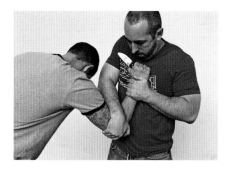

Once the knife has been pulled down and is pressed against your body, slide your hand over your assailant's elbow so that you are able to control and move their arm.

Start to straighten their arm by turning your body and pulling with both hands—one pulling your attacker's wrist, and the other their elbow. You can use this movement to drive your assailant into the wall.

Keep turning and bring your armpit up and over your assailant's knife arm, and bring your weight down on it. Rather than press straight down, lean into your assailant to keep their body down and pressed up against the wall, restricting their movement.

Release your right hand (the one that was on their elbow joint), making sure you maintain weight and pressure on your assailant. In reality, you will slide your hand along the arm, so it can renew the grip at any time, should your attacker struggle. For clarity the photo shows the hand being "cleanly" removed.

Grab your assailant's wrist and lower your elbow to your side. The closer your limbs are to your body, the stronger your hold will be. Try to close the space between you and your assailant as much as possible, as this will limit the room they have to maneuver.

Once you have a firm grip on their wrist, slide your other arm under your attacker's knife arm to wrap round and grip on to your own wrist. You now have your assailant's knife arm in a solid "figure four" lock. Although there are several hand changes to get to this position, if you keep your assailant's arm locked to your body and your weight pressed into them, the knife arm won't be able to move.

You are now in a position to use your assailant's knife against them. There is little point in simply holding a control or lock in a real-life situation—rather, you should be looking to end the incident as quickly and conclusively as possible.

In a circular motion, start to turn the attacker's knife towards them. This should be a relatively "tight" movement and your body should push the knife arm, rather then rely on your arm strength to do this. Moving in this manner, as well as being a stronger movement, creates less space for your assailant to try to escape or redirect the movement.

Keep turning and moving the knife towards your assailant's neck—you have a choice, depending on the length of the blade, to stab them directly in the throat, or to slash them across the side of the neck (on the carotid artery).

Using your body to push, keep turning the knife towards your attacker.

Slash them across the side of the throat; once again your fingerprints are not on the knife, and it is clear who the instigator of the situation was. If we are dealing with someone who is prepared to use a knife against us, we should not enter the conflict without being prepared to do the same. Survival at all costs has to be your priority.

Gun Threat Against a Wall

In this scenario, your assailant has pushed you up against a wall and stuck a gun to your throat. Grab the barrel of the gun with both hands and turn it towards your attacker. At the same time, make a body defense by pulling your head back towards the wall to the side of the weapon, and out of the line of fire.

You should keep pushing down on the gun and rotating it, to open the hand that is holding it. Once you've freed it, you can use the gun as an impact weapon.

When you are pushed up against a wall and a gun is put to your face, making a good body defense can be very difficult, and so the hand defense component of the technique becomes key. Raise your hands up level with the weapon—this will meet your assailant's expectations of how you should react in such a scenario.

Move your head to the side as much as you can to try to get out of the line of fire, while grabbing the gun with both hands. Your thumbs should grip under the barrel as close to the trigger guard as possible. If the firearm has a small frame, one of your hands will have to grip over the trigger guard (see the position of the left hand in the next photo).

Using the barrel for leverage, rapidly turn the gun towards your assailant. If your assailant already has their finger on the trigger, do not be surprised if the gun goes off in this position. If you are dealing with a revolver, your hands will probably get burnt if this happens (with a revolver, the hot gasses that propel the bullet escape through, and around the frame).

Continue turning the gun towards your assailant until they are unable to keep hold of it.

Now smash the weapon repeatedly into your attacker's face, driving them backwards. As well as taking them out of the fight with your strikes, you should aim to create enough space to move away from the wall and disengage. It would be dangerous to assume that there are no friends or third parties in the environment that could assist your attacker.

Consequences of Actions

Every time you hit or punch somebody, you cause them to move (either backwards, downwards, etc.). If you punch someone while they are hold-ing a weapon, you will force them backwards, and in all likelihood they will take with them the weapon that you were trying to control. As your arm extends, so your level of control decreases. There are times to punch and strike your assailant while disarming or controlling a weapon, but you must be aware that every action you take has a consequence, and if punching causes movement that lessens your control of the weapon, it should be avoided.

When performing a disarm, there are certainly times when striking and punching are advisable. However, you should be aware that if you punch a person with a firearm without following their movement—i.e., when you punch them, you stay where you are—you are likely to move them backwards, with the gun still in their possession.

If there is a good deal of distance between you and your attacker, and they are holding their weapon with arms extended, you may find it difficult to close the distance in order to deliver solid strikes.

If your assailant has a two-handed grip on the gun and you are only controlling it with one, they may be able to turn the gun back towards you, putting you back in the line of fire.

If your punch is powerful enough, it may knock the person off their feet, and as they fall they may pull the gun with them. It will be hard to keep hold of the barrel as the gun is pulled downwards, and if the gun's sight rips/cuts across your palm, there can be an instinctual reaction to let go of your hold.

If you are dealing with someone who has been trained in weapon retention, they may be able to pull away from you and drop to the ground, re-training the weapon on you. Getting both hands to the gun as soon as possible is the safest way of ensuring that you disarm your assailant. Striking an attacker holding a weapon should be limited to certain situations.

In an incident involving a knife, the greatest weapon you will have is the knife itself, and your time and effort would be best spent looking at how to use this weapon against your attacker, rather than simply striking them.

If a person holding a gun has been trained in any form of weapon retention, they may try to drop to the ground as a better means of holding on to their weapon. If you punch or strike them as part of your disarm, you may be helping them get to the ground faster.

"Steaming" and "Steamers"

In every aggressive and violent situation you face, you should make three assumptions regarding your assailant:

1. They are armed, even if a weapon isn't evident—and even if they've been previously disarmed (they may always have a back-up weapon).
2. There are third parties in the environment who can come to the assistance of your assailant(s).
3. Your assailant has the competence to deal with any defense you make.

In certain situations, it will be very clear that you are dealing with an armed group, rather than a single armed assailant. One very particular form of mugging is "steaming." This usually involves a large, armed group who use intimidation through numbers, as well as weapons, to force compliance. Often, they will work in transit stations and on trains, buses, etc., selecting victims and then crowding round them to disguise the mugging that is going on in the center.

If you are walking and see a group that was together "fan out" before you, you can be pretty sure that they are planning to surround you (this is a natural pre-violence indicator). In such situations, look to change your direction and leave the environment as quickly as possible. While the primary motive of the group may be financial, it is impossible to determine the secondary motives of individuals within the group (do they want to injure or even kill you to increase their standing within the gang?). Group aggression and violence is volatile, especially if members have been taking drugs or drinking before going out on a mugging spree or "steaming."

A group walking directly towards you have synchronized their movement to yours and should be considered a threat. (Not every group will be so obvious in indicating their harmful intent towards you.) When groups of individuals intend to assault you, one of the first movements they make is to "fan out"— you should be aware of what this looks like and what it means.

A group who are intending to commit a crime against you will start to spread or "fan out," making it difficult for you to get past them. They are effectively looking to cut off your exit and escape routes.

The group here has spread out, blocking the way ahead.

They continue to move in order to surround you, and block off your exit routes.

Although your first thought in any mugging scenario should be to comply, if your assailant(s) remain at the scene after you have acquiesced to their demands, you will need to think about making a physical defense—whatever the odds against you. You should be honest and realistic here, and recognize that you are acting because you have no choice.

Knife to Same Side of Throat

Oftentimes, when a person knows there are people with and around them, their actions become emboldened, and if they believe the group they are with will hide their actions, they may make a more visible and aggressive threat. If your primary assailant has a knife positioned against your throat and, after handing over the wallet, they and the group remain, you will need to make a physical defense, as your mugger is now likely considering using the knife against you.

With both hands, grab your assailant's knife hand (with your thumbs on the back of their wrist), and pull down, rolling it against your chest (away from your neck) before explosively pushing it towards your assailant's neck, with the intent of cutting them. You should step forward, to assist your push. You can also lock your arms out, if necessary, so that if your assailant tries to resist, they will be unable to bring the knife back to your throat.

Straight away, swing your right leg back and use this movement to drag the knife across your assailant's throat. If there is someone behind you, you can deliver an elbow strike as you step back and bring the knife to your hip. Immediately thread your left arm under your assailant's knife arm. Rather than make a stabbing motion to their side, bring the knife up to their throat with your right hand and put your left hand behind their head. They are now your hostage.

Now disengage, taking them with you—and telling the rest of the group to back off.

A group have managed to isolate and surround you, and one member has put a knife to your throat. (In reality, the others will stand close in order to shield/hide whatever assault is about to occur.) If the demand is for your wallet, phone, etc, hand it over. If the group stay after you acquiesce, or they try to move you to another location, you will need to respond with a physical solution.

Immediately pluck the knife from your throat with your left hand, rolling it down from your neck and onto your chest. Bring your right hand to the assailant's knife hand and pin their hand to your chest. At this point stop pulling down and pull in towards you to lock the knife hand to your chest.

Understand that in this position, you have not been able to get your thumbs to the back of your attacker's knife hand, and the control comes from you pinning the knife, with pressure to your chest.

Start to bring your chest over your attacker's hand so that their wrist is forced to bend. As you do this, move your thumbs onto the back of your assailant's hand, and continue to bend the hand back towards the wrist.

Using your body, and extending your arms, start to drive the knife back towards your attacker. (Your body can assist in this movement.)

Bring the knife to your attacker's throat and slash it across the side of their neck. You need to send a quick and clear message to the rest of the group, showing what you are prepared to do to anyone that tries to assault you. You should try to cause the others to hesitate and think about the possible consequences of their actions, so that they are paralysed into inaction.

After cutting your assailant's neck, pull the knife down to your hips.

Thread your left arm under your assailant's elbow.

Start to drive your hips into your attacker, directing the knife so that it is pointing towards them.

Complete the hip thrust by driving the knife into your attacker's side.

Although you have dealt with one assailant, you have not dealt with the others. In order to avoid having to, you should look to take your attacker "hostage." Move the arm that was under the attacker's elbow to the back of their neck and start to bring the knife up to the side of their throat.

Keep moving the knife towards their throat, while controlling them with your other hand.

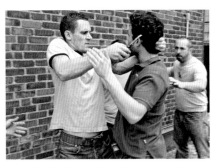

You should now have one hand on the back of their neck, your forearm pressed against one side of their neck, and the knife pushed against the other. Your attacker is now in your complete control.

Tell the rest of the group to stay back or you will kill their friend. They have already seen you slash and stab him, so they should have no reason not to believe you would fulfill your threat. Back away until you are at a safe distance to disengage, then push away your attacker and go. You can leave them still holding the knife, as they will be in no condition to follow you.

If any members of the group try to stop you or get involved, use the attacker who you have "hostage" to block or impede their movement.

Gun to Front of Head

If your assailant believes they are unseen or have the cover of the group, they may not try to conceal the gun, but hold it high to the head. If they are drunk or on drugs, they may be less concerned as to the consequences of their actions, such as getting caught, and are therefore prepared to make more dramatic and obvious threats. When dealing with an erratic person who may be drugged up, and looks to have little control of the gun, your best solution may be to perform a disarm, without waiting to find out what the demand being made of you is, so as to avoid the trigger being pulled accidentally.

This technique works well at almost any height, from midsection to head; however, it comes into its own at about solar-plexus level and above. One thing you should always try to do with a weapon disarm is to keep your hands at the height of the wrist(s) in which the weapon is being held (if it is a low threat, the hands should be low; if it's a high threat, they should be high, etc.). Once the weapon comes above the solar plexus, the hands naturally change from being able to grip underhand and are limited to making an overhand grip, making the underhand defenses described earlier difficult to execute at this height.

Putting your hands up is a natural response to having a weapon pointed at you, and one that your assailant will expect. That said, if you are told to put your hands down, you should do so—or immediately attempt a disarm. If you have to disarm from "a hands down" position, the body defense part of your technique becomes the primary means of initial defense, and may need to be exaggerated to compensate for the imperfect hand position.

First, "cry yourself into position"—this will involve putting your hands up, and possibly moving forward somewhat to bring yourself within arms-reach of the gun. Don't exaggerate this, as it may alert your assailant to your intentions—you may want to offer them your wallet as you move forward, as if you are only moving nearer in order to hand it to them. This may also interrupt their "script," because if they were intending to abduct you, sexually assault you, or even kill you, they will at least have to process this new information, and this may cause them to hesitate.

Don't wiggle your fingers or make any movement with your hands that could draw your assailant's attention to them and their close proximity to the weapon. You want to paint a big picture that meets your assailant's expectations of what such a situation should look like— and one that they probably visualized before carrying out the assault; one where you're scared and your hands are up. What you don't want to do is draw their attention to particular details, which is what any unnecessary movements around the weapon may do.

When you are dealing with any threats to the front, don't look directly into, or at, your assailant's face. If they believe that you will be able to identify them later, they may decide to kill you on the spot, eliminating a potential witness to their crime. This may seem extreme, but if your assailant has a criminal record and is destined to go back to prison for a long period of time if they break the terms of their parole, they may deem it worthwhile to take you out of the picture. You never know the history of the person you are dealing with.

Tell them that you have money. Ask them if they want you to hand it over to them, or if they want to come and take it themselves. Basically, you are causing them to think and make decisions, which means they are having to become more rational and therefore less emotional, at the same time creating the opportunity for you to prepare for your disarm. This may mean shifting your weight to get into a better stance, position, etc. Asking these questions will also cause them to focus on what you are saying, rather than on your hands, which are getting ready to take the gun. The more information you give them to process, the less likely they are to be focused on retaining the weapon.

To make your hand defense, move your hand to the gun by pivoting on your toes (the body always moves the arms). For the body defense, turn to the side, "blading" the body and leaning your weight back—don't take a step, as this would mean making a large body movement that your assailant might respond to by tracking their weapon as you move (you should aim to turn inside your own silhouette). By "blading" the body, you will move it out of the line of fire, and make yourself a smaller target.

Grab the barrel of the gun firmly, as close to the trigger guard as possible. At the same time, your other hand should come up to the back of the gun, where the hammer is.

Rather than bringing the gun down, keep it at the same level, but turn it. This simple action moves the barrel of the gun away from the center of your mass to the peripheries, which, if shot, are less likely to be fatal.

Pull the gun vigorously as your body continues to turn (the whole movement should be explosive and powered by the body's movement), to bring the gun past you. This should also upset the assailant's balance, negating both their grab reflex and any attempts at retention.

Turn the barrel towards them, and pull with the right hand, ripping the gun from their grip. If they are persistent at holding on—though the speed with which you pulled the gun should have dealt with this—you can drive your forearm into their wrist to bend their hand back and open the grip.

Rather than attacking your primary assailant with the frame of the gun, use it against those in the group who are blocking your exit route.

In this situation, you are facing an assailant who is holding a gun to your head. Put your hands up in a passive, non-aggressive fashion. Your assailants have watched enough movies to assume this is a natural response to having a gun pointed at you.

Start to turn your body, and reach with your left hand to take a grip of the barrel of the gun. Grab as close to the trigger guard as you can.

Continue your turn, moving the gun away from you, and moving your body out of the line of fire. Your other hand should reach towards where the hammer/rear sight of the gun is, and cup the back of the weapon.

The gun should now be turned flat on its side. This simple action turns the barrel an extra few inches away from you. If the gun goes off while you have hold of the slide (this applies only to semi-automatic weapons), although it will fire, the slide will not be able to pull back and eject the spent casing and so pull a new bullet into the chamber, jamming the gun.

Keep turning, and pulling the gun past you. If you do this rapidly as part of your initial movement, you will beat your attacker's natural grab reflex (to pull back in an attempt to retain whunatever it is that is being pulled from them), and may in fact release the gun from their hand.

Keep pulling, and at the same time start to turn the firearm towards your attacker. Your pull should be strong enough that it takes your assailant's balance—when a person's balance is taken, all their thoughts go to regaining it, and they don't think about or focus on anything else, i.e., holding on to their weapon, etc.

Your pulling and turning action should force your attacker to let go. If they have a strong grip and you are experiencing difficulties, use your left forearm (the arm which is holding the barrel of the gun) to drive downwards into your attacker's wrist to help expedite the release.

As you drive your forearm into their wrist, rotate it so you weaken their hold. Your end position should see your assailant off balance and in a disadvantaged position.

Now you have the weapon in your hand.

Immediately use the gun as an impact weapon to cause blunt trauma to your assailant(s).

You should now disengage. If you do intend to use the weapon as a firearm, you may need to clear any stoppages, and ensure that it is entirely operational. This is best done from a distance. Keep the weapon close to you so that it is difficult for any passerby to see, and easy for you to retain should any member of the group attempt to disarm you.

Abductions and Hostage Taking

A predator will take you hostage if they believe you have a worth/value to somebody else. This may involve moving you from one location to another. If you happen to be present during a robbery at a convenience store, bank, or similar business, which the police interrupt, it may be that you are taken hostage, so that the criminal can use you to leverage an advantage from the authorities. Hostage taking doesn't always have to be planned or premeditated, but can happen in a spontaneous fashion. If you travel abroad to countries where foreigners from your country are targeted by criminal gangs or terrorist groups, you may be directly targeted due to your profile. It could be that your captor's motivations are criminal—they want a ransom—or it could be that they want to use you as a bargaining chip to force political, military, or religious change or concessions.

An abduction involves you being moved from a "primary" location to a "secondary" one, either as a hostage (where you have a perceived value to somebody else), or as someone who has value to the person abducting you, e.g., they want to sexually assault you. There are two things to note about abductions:

1. The location you are in represents your best chance of dealing with the threat (one of the reasons your abductor is trying to remove you from it);

2. You have value to your abductor (otherwise they would have hurt or killed you immediately).

While it generally makes sense to acquiesce to a mugger's demands for your property (wallet, mobile phone, laptop, etc.), it rarely makes sense to go along with someone who is trying to forcibly move you to another location.

It is important to understand that 99.9 percent of the time, your best time to act and escape is in the first moments of an attempted abduction. There will never be a perfect time to escape, but the moment of capture, or when you are initially being moved, generally represents the time you are most likely to be successful. This is for the following reasons:

1. Your assailant(s) will be at their least prepared at the start of any confrontation. Every piece of their plan that they complete successfully will add to their confidence and reinforce their control of the situation. Conversely, every failure will cause them to rethink their plan, making them more unpredictable and emotionally volatile. Time rarely works in the favor of the hostage or abductee. If there is more than one person involved in the abduction, they will be at their least organized and coordinated at the initial moment of the assault.

2. The more time that passes, the less worth you will have to your captor(s). Over time, most hostage takers realize that their initial demands will not be met, and that they will have to settle for less than they first bargained for. This directly equates to a decrease in your worth and value to them. At the initial moment of the assault, however, your assailant(s) will be more concerned about putting their plan into action, rather than hurting you or despatching you, as you still have worth.

3. As human beings, we like to avoid confrontation and doing anything that may put us in danger. By not acting in the moment of seizure, we are reinforcing this behavior, and convincing ourselves that a better opportunity to act will present itself later. It is unlikely that this will be the case. In an abduction scenario, the reason you are moved from one location to another is because the one you are in is the least beneficial for your abductor (which makes it the most advantageous place for you to make your escape).

Just like muggers, abductors will use crowds and busy places to obscure their activities, as well as to synchronize their movement with you. Sticking a knife in your back and telling you to walk, while holding your arm, is both a discrete and unexpected way of moving you—both to you and those around you. This type of abduction is much more likely than that of a car pulling up and you being dragged inside it, which would cause a noticeable spectacle. Whatever the nature of the assault, your best time to act and fight is in that moment—rather than waiting for a better time that is unlikely to come.

Rear Hostage Knife to Front of Throat

If you let an assailant know where you are heading, you present them with an easy opportunity to synchronize their movement to yours. Telling someone over a mobile phone where you are going, what you are doing, and where you may be at a particular time will allow any predatory individual listening an easy opportunity to join their movement to yours. (You don't even have to be speaking loudly; in fact, speaking softly can often cause people in your environment to listen harder to what you are saying.) If you use the remote key fob to locate your car in a parking lot, you will be announcing to anyone in the environment where you are heading, as well as unlocking the one place you had that was locked and safe. It may be that while you are walking to your car, someone comes up behind you and puts a knife to your throat, telling you to move.

When this happens, you should immediately bring your hands together to form a "hook." Keep your elbows at your side, so that the assailant can't see your arms when they move up towards the knife arm. You should raise your "hook" above the knife hand and pluck down explosively. The first action of yours that your assailant should be aware of is their knife hand being pulled down—don't place your hands on the arm and then pull down, as they will know as soon as you try to grab them that you are about to make a defense.

You should make a body defense by throwing your head back into your attacker and pulling your throat away from the knife.

Once the knife is away from your throat, press your attacker's hand firmly into your chest, as this is a direction your assailant won't be able to pull against (don't pull down any further once the knife is clear of your neck—you are for the moment safe from this threat, as you have two hands on the knife and are using your body to help control it).

Using the bottom hand of your hook, move your thumb around your assailant's wrist so that you are holding it. Keeping the knife hand pressed to your chest, raise your shoulder and step under your attacker's arm, transferring the top hand of your hook to be under your assailant's hand. You should now be behind them with their knife pointing into them. Step into the attacker, using your body to push the knife toward them. Do this repeatedly, if necessary.

Now disengage and run—your assailant may have accomplices in the area working with them.

It is easy to be task-focused and unaware, e.g., you have finished work and just want to get to your car and go home. When exiting a building you should look right and left, just as you would when crossing a road. If you had in this instance, you would have identified that a person was waiting for something/someone.

This person turns out to be an assailant/abductor, who synchronizes their movement to yours by following you, and places a knife to your throat. When somebody wants to move you from one location to another, you need to put a physical solution in place. The fact that they need to move you somewhere else to commit the assault means your best chance of survival is in this location.

Immediately form your hands into a single hook. As well as utilizing the strength of both arms, this hook will force you to keep your arms by your side, which will minimize the amount of movement you will have to make before you take the knife, and so give your assailant little time to react or respond.

Raise your two hands (the "hook") over your assailant's weapon arm. It is important that you don't simply put your hands on it, as this will alert them to the fact that you are about to make some form of disarm. The first thing they should feel is your hands moving the knife away.

Explosively pluck down onto the knife hand/arm. Your aggressor should have no opportunity to respond as the knife is pulled away from your throat. As soon as you have cleared the weapon, pull it into your chest.

Keeping the knife hand locked to your chest, start to turn under your assailant's arm. You can raise your shoulder to help lift the arm up, so you don't have to bend down too much.

It is important to keep the knife hand pinned to your body as you turn, as this restricts your assailant's arm movement and prevents them, however strong, from pulling it free. As long as you keep the knife clasped to you, they may be able to move you around, but they won't be able to get the knife free.

Slide your top hand down so it is positioned under the attacker's knife hand. Move your head so it is behind your assailant's arm, and keep their wrist locked to your chest. The knife should now be pointed towards your attacker.

Keeping the knife pressed tightly to your chest...

...Use your body to explosively drive the knife into your assailant's side.

The Denial, Deliberation, and Decision Loop

It may be that as you walk to your car you hear footsteps behind you and you become adrenalized, aware that someone is following you. Unfortunately, most people go into a state of denial when this happens, convincing themselves that their fear system has over-reacted and that they are in no real danger. If they do accept that their adrenal system was triggered for a reason, they will then deliberate on what to do, eventually reaching a decision and then possibly acting on it. If a person who is following you is intent on causing you harm, this lengthy process will more than likely be interrupted by their attack.

You should have pre-built responses to certain situations, such as being followed, where you immediately turn around and ask the person in your wake if they are following you, etc. If the person following you did have a harmful intent towards you and planned to abduct you, you have now interrupted their "script" and they are likely to abort their plan. If the person had just fallen into step with you, it is highly unlikely they will act violently towards your question.

When people first recognize that they may be in danger (through their subconscious adrenal/fear system), they usually go into a state of denial, explaining to themselves why the threat they've picked up on isn't really a threat. They then enter a stage of deliberation, trying frantically to reach a decision/come up with a solution to their situation. Krav Maga teaches people to bypass this lengthy process and act decisively.

It is natural for people to go into denial and a physical state of freezing—it is how quickly you come out of these states that determines your survival chances.

Protecting Third Parties—Rear Hostage to Front of Throat

Sometimes the person needing protection isn't you, and you are called upon to protect a third party, such as a friend or family member. You may now need to perform disarms and weapon controls on behalf of another.

If you are going to attempt to control or disarm somebody who is threatening another person, you will need to get yourself into a position where, with one step or movement, you are able to close the distance and execute some form of control. If you have to move first, and then move again to make a control/disarm, the assailant will be given too much warning.

As with any threat situation, you can engage the assailant in conversation both before and during the time you execute your physical response. If the attacker is focused on what you are saying, they are less likely to be concentrating on your movement.

Move to a position where the assailant's sight lines are somewhat restricted—you can cover your movement by telling the attacker that you are moving away. If you can use your partner's head to hide your hand movement, this will be to both of your advantages.

Keep your hands up, maintaining an interview/de-escalation stance. This will allow your hands to be closer to the knife and increase your chances of taking control of your assailant's weapon arm.

Don't hook your hands together—you will want to maximize your chances of hooking the attacker's knife arm, and using both hands will double your chances of accomplishing this.

With one movement, step forward and hook the knife arm down and to the side, away from your partner's neck. With your right hand, strongly pull down as you step to your left and past your partner.

Now thread your left arm under the attacker's elbow and position the knife onto your hip, and thrust explosively upwards to stab them in their side.

There are five situational components that any violent situation is composed of:
1. The Location;
2. Your relationship with the attacker;
3. The attacker's motive;
4. Your state of mind/preparedness;
5. Third parties who are with you. You may not be the target/victim of an act of violence; instead, the person being assaulted may be a friend or other third party.

When we are with other people and/or in crowds, our natural levels of awareness drop, as we by default start to rely on those around us to identify potential threats and dangers. In this instance, both of you have failed to pick up someone in your environment, or recognize that they have synchronized their movement to yours (in this case, they are following you).

This time, the knife threat is made to the person you are with. The attacker places a knife to their throat and starts to pull them away.

Adopt an Interview Stance and ask the abductor what they want. Ask open-ended questions that will force them to think about their answers. By keeping them talking you are getting them to focus more on what you are saying, and less on what they are doing.

If you can—and it is natural in this situation—try to move so that the hostage's head is between you and the abductor. If you can obscure their sight lines, you have a much better chance of accomplishing your goal.

It is very easy to hesitate, and talk yourself out of performing a technique. However, to be successful in such a situation, you need to be decisive. Have a question in mind that you can ask your assailant, such as "Is there anything I can do to help resolve this?" Time your movement to begin as you say the word "help"—this is a good technique to force yourself to act, and catches the assailant off-guard, as they should still be processing the question.

Driving forward, grab the assailant's knife arm with both hands—don't use a single hook, as you want to maximize your chances of getting hold of the knife arm.

With both hands, pull the abductor's knife arm down and away from your friend and towards your body. If your friend is frozen with fear, you may need to shout to them at this stage to move and go, as they may not be capable of doing this without instruction.

Pull the knife down towards your hips.

Then thread your arm around your assailant's, and clasp it to your body.

You can make your clasp more secure by grabbing on to your own clothing—this can be especially important if your skin is slippery due to sweat. In Israel, it is often hard to hold on to a limb by grip alone, due to the sweat on a person's arm. Using clothing to restrict movement is a good way to overcome this.

Now drive your hips towards the abductor, stabbing them in the side with their own knife. Your fingerprints should not be on the knife.

Rear Knife Threat—Knife to Side of Throat

In this situation, the knife is to the side of your throat. If you were to pull down on the knife in the same way as you did when the knife was to the front of your throat, you would end up cutting your own throat. In this instance, you must first clear the knife away from the side of your throat.

Make a hand defense by explosively pushing your attacker's elbow to the side—the first thing your attacker should feel is their arm being moved (not your hand being placed upon it). Your initial body defense will be to move your neck to the side, away from the knife.

As your right hand pushes the arm across, your left hand should come up and clasp your assailant's arm to your chest. Pull in towards you, rather than down. Keep your left elbow and arm pressed to your side, as this gives your arm the best mechanical advantage.

The hand that was pushing the elbow should now slide to the back of your head so that you have your assailant's upper arm trapped between your neck and your bicep. Raise the shoulder and step under your assailant's knife arm, keeping everything locked in position.

As you start to move behind them, bring the arm that was locking your assailant's upper arm under their elbow and move the hand nearest to the knife to control their hand—this should be placed on the knife. Now stab violently upwards into your assailant's body.

If a person is holding a knife to the front of your throat, pulling it straight down is a good solution.

If the knife is to the side of the neck, pulling straight down would end up cutting an artery. In this situation, the knife needs to be pushed to the side first, away from the neck.

To move the knife away from the side of your neck, explosively push on your assailant's elbow to move their forearm across your neck, taking their hand/knife away from your neck. At the same time, start to bring your other arm up, ready to secure the hand/wrist holding the knife. You should have in your head the idea of the hand on the elbow, pushing the arm across to "feed" the attacker's knife hand/wrist to your other hand.

Your end position should see the knife pushed away from your neck, and your left hand pinning the knife arm to your chest.

The hand that pushed the elbow should now be brought behind your head.

Your goal is to pin your assailant's upper arm between your head and your own upper arm. This, coupled with the pin you have on their knife hand/wrist, means that their weapon arm is locked securely in place and is unable to move. You should now begin to step under your attacker's weapon arm.

Keep turning under your assailant's arm, while at the same time sliding your right arm down...

...So it can clasp your attacker's arm at the elbow joint.

Pull the knife back towards your hips, and position the knife so that it is pointed towards your attacker.

Then use your hips to drive the knife upwards and into your attacker.

Knife to Side of Neck

Your assailant may not come at you from the rear, but from the side. They may wait for you to pass a place where they are hiding and then step out as you pass, putting a knife to your throat.

In almost all instances where threats of this nature take place, the point of the knife will be upwards and the handle down, as this allows the holder to pull the knife down in order to make the cut (the knife being held the other way is unusual, because the attacker would have to pull the knife away from themselves in order to slit your throat).

You should immediately bring your hands up, keeping them close to your neck and your assailant's wrist. Don't make contact, but keep them close. You can turn the palm of your furthest hand to face your assailant's knife hand in preparation for the control that you are going to execute.

Tuck your chin down and place it close to the hand that is holding the knife (but don't make contact, as this may alert your attacker that you are preparing to act). You can use your chin to push the knife away from your neck if your assailant starts to drag the blade across it before you have time to make a proper defense. It is important to understand that this is an insurance policy, and should not form your primary defense.

Turn on the toes of the foot furthest away, moving your right hand/wrist into your attacker's arm. This action will also pull your neck away from the blade, giving you a combined hand and body defense.

With your second hand, grab their wrist. Immediately turn the hand that made the block, so it can also grab your assailant's knife arm. This will give you two hands on the knife arm.

If your assailant is holding on to your shoulder, push the knife over their arm and direct the blade so that it cuts/slices into their bicep—keep doing this repeatedly until they release their grip. Knife slashes have a similar feel to electric shocks, and produce a similar response, i.e., pulling away.

Now step out to your left and violently pull the knife hand down to your hips. Move your left arm under the elbow and hug the arm to your body. You are now in a position from which you can stab your assailant, using the same upward hip thrust described in previous techniques.

When you walk past corners, you should try to clear them with enough room so that you won't be surprised if somebody is waiting/hiding out of sight.

Understand that most threats/attacks happen with movement. An assailant will often move you while they make a demand, so that you will be overwhelmed with trying to manage your footwork and won't think about fighting back.

Immediately bring your hands up. You should also try to drop your chin down so that the knife isn't pressing directly into your neck.

Start to turn, moving the knife away from your neck with the hand/arm nearest the attacker's weapon arm. This movement will also pull your neck away from the knife, providing both a hand and body defense.

With your other hand, grab the wrist of your assailant's weapon arm.

The hand that initially moved the knife out of the way should now turn and grab the hand holding the knife. You should now have one hand on the attacker's wrist and another on the hand holding the blade.

Step to the side, pulling the knife arm vigorously down. Use your body weight, not just your arm strength.

Release your grip on their wrist, keeping hold of the hand holding the knife.

Now thread your arm under your assailant's elbow (the hand holding the knife should be pinned to your hips).

Using the full force of your body, drive forward and upwards with your hips, stabbing your aggressor with their own knife. At no point should your fingerprints be on the weapon.

Gun to Side of Head

Your attacker may choose to use a gun to the side of your head, instead of a knife. The basic movements to deal with this are the same.

First, turn on the toes of the foot furthest away from the weapon, moving your right hand/wrist into your attacker's arm. This action will also pull your head away from the gun.

With your second hand, grab the barrel of the gun (don't use the thumb to grip with, as this may cause you to muzzle your hand with the gun).

Keep control of the attacker's wrist and pivot so that your body is facing your assailant.

Now punch the gun away while pulling the wrist back, in a similar fashion to the release you executed in the Gun to Front of Body disarm (see pages 66–68). Then strike your assailant repeatedly with the firearm.

In this instance, the assailant has a gun, rather than a knife. It could be that they have been conducting surveillance on the premises over a period of time, and know exactly when certain people enter and exit the building. If somebody follows a regular routine, a potential assailant will know where they will be at any moment during the day.

An assailant steps out, pointing a gun at you.

Put up your hands. This is something they will expect you to do, and will greatly increase your chances of controlling and disarming the weapon. If the assailant had simply wanted to shoot you, they could have done so as you passed them. The fact that they want you to see the weapon means they intend to intimidate you and/or force you to comply with their demands.

Start to turn, moving the gun away from you with your nearest hand. This hand and body movement should remove you from the line of fire.

Your other hand should grab the attacker's wrist and take control of it.

The hand that initially moved the gun away from your head should now grab it. You should have one hand on their wrist and one hand on the gun.

Start to turn towards your attacker, pulling on their wrist, and punching through with the gun.

Pull on the wrist, and punch through with the gun. Power will come through weight transference (back leg to front leg), sinking of the hips, and chaining the movements of the legs, hips, back, shoulder, and arms together in one motion.

After you have disarmed the weapon, use it as an impact tool to inflict maximum concussive force on your assailant.

Do not rely on just one strike, but repeatedly strike them with the gun. This is the most reliable way to use the firearm as a weapon, as you do not know if it is operational (it could be jammed, empty/unloaded, the safety on, etc.).

Using the Body to Assist Against a Resisting Assailant

There are times when a quick release of the gun isn't possible, and where the body needs to be fully employed in order for a successful disarm to take place. This can occur because the assailant has responded to your initial disarm by tightening their grip on the weapon, and locking their wrist. This type of response is rare, because most attackers aren't expecting their victim to fight back, especially when the odds seem so stacked against them. This is one of the advantages of raising the hands in a submissive fashion—it causes your assailant to believe you are not a threat.

From the initial position of one hand on the gun and one on the wrist, circle your left arm over to secure the gun under your armpit. If the gun was fired when you first grabbed it, it will be jammed if it is a semiautomatic (this is one of the advantages of grabbing the barrel and restricting the sliding motion that ejects the casing); if it is a revolver, it will probably burn your hand and be ready to fire again.

Trap the gun under your armpit with your assailant's hand pressed firmly to your chest. Join your left hand to your right forearm and drop your elbows, squeezing everything together and taking all the space away. Now rapidly turn to your left and rip the gun free.

There are times when you try to perform the disarm shown above, only to realize your attacker has such a strong grip on the weapon that you won't be able to release it in the usual fashion. This is rare, but you should have a solution to this problem if you encounter it.

Start to perform the regular gun to the side of the head disarm.

After trying to release the gun by pushing with the right hand and pulling with the left, you realize your assailant's grip is too strong.

Rather than struggling with the same release, swing your elbow over your assailant's weapon arm. It will help you pull your assailant's gun away from them.

Continue to pull your elbow over, with the aim of trapping your attacker's wrist in the crook of your elbow.

Keep turning—your goal is to not just restrict wrist movement, but hand movement, as well.

Your attacker's gun hand should not be able to move at all. If they can turn their firearm one degree to the left or right, you are not close enough to their hand, and should pull yourself forward.

Squeeze the weapon hand as if you are applying a choke to the wrist (squeezing the forearm and bicep together, and bringing the elbows together). Turn rapidly towards your attacker. This movement should start to open the grip of the attacker's hand on the weapon.

Keep turning with the body, while rotating the barrel of the gun towards your assailant.

This will open your assailant's hand up and allow you to disarm them of their weapon.

Rear Hostage with Gun to Head

Abductions aren't always planned, and people who take hostages often don't have a clear idea of what the goals and aims of their actions are. The husband who kidnaps his ex-wife, or the person who takes a passerby hostage during an interrupted robbery at a convenience store, often do so without any clear plan in mind. This is in contrast to a criminal or terrorist group, who take hostages for financial or political reward.

You may be shopping in a convenience store when a robbery begins to take place. In the course of it, the robber hears police sirens and, in a panic, grabs you as a hostage. The gun that was being used to force the shop owner to hand over the money in the till is now trained on you, while they use their other arm to move you in front of them as a protective shield. This arm will also be used to control your movement.

Your defense will largely depend on how your attacker is controlling your body, whether by holding you across the chest, which will restrict your ability to turn, or by holding your neck, which will allow your body to move more freely.

Rear Hostage with Arm Around Neck

As soon as the gun is pointed at your head, bring both hands up. This is an action your abductor will expect you to make. Your hand which is furthest away can be turned so that your palm is facing the gun—this won't be noticed by your assailant as your head will obscure their vision.

It would be easy to imagine that you're not high profile enough to be the victim of an abduction or hostage-taking. However, circumstances can determine your value to an assailant. You may be present at a crime scene/incident, where a criminal decides that their best option in the situation is to take a hostage.

Imagine that you are at a convenience store when an armed robbery takes place. At first, you are simply a bystander witnessing the crime. As the robber is committing their crime they hear a police cruiser go by and assume that this is related. In a panic, they grab you to use as a bargaining chip.

Your first response will probably be one of denial, i.e., this can't be happening to me. The first step in ensuring your survival is to accept the reality of what is happening, and realize that it is up to you to find a solution to your situation.

The first thing to do when a gun is pointed at your head is to raise your hands. This is something your assailant expects you to do. By raising your hands up, you'll also be able to ascertain how much control your attacker has of your upper body.

If you can raise the hand furthest from the gun all the way up, you will be able to turn your body. Raise the hand farthest from the gun all the way up (if you are able), and turn your body towards your attacker. Move the hand farthest from the gun towards the barrel.

Grab the barrel and smash the gun into their face, while at the same time dropping your other arm down and under their elbow. If your attacker has their finger on the trigger and it goes off in this position, they will shoot themselves in the face. You may perforate your own eardrum, but you will have solved your larger problem.

Wherever possible, you should try to turn an attacker's weapon towards them (ideally using it against them). If your assailant now has a gun pointed towards them, they have a problem to solve, not you. You can now focus on being the aggressor. You should continue to move your right arm past and behind the elbow of their weapon arm.

Keep turning and driving the gun into your assailant's face. You are now the attacker, not them, and this is an important mental shift to make. Maintaining the role of victim will not help you survive this incident.

Once you have positioned your left hand behind your assailant's elbow, bring it up to take hold of the gun. You should now have two hands on the weapon, with your attacker's arm in an entangled arm lock. They will find it very difficult to hold on to the gun in this position.

Start to rotate the gun. Your right hand should turn the barrel downwards. This will cause your assailant to lose their grip and release the weapon.

By continuing to rotate the gun, you will disarm your attacker.

Now strike them with it, until they no longer remain a threat.

Turn on the ball of your left foot, so that you can bring your left hand to the gun, and grab hold of it, turning the barrel away from your head. Your aim should be to smash the gun into your assailant's face with this movement.

The turning motion will also pull your head away from the line of fire—this is your body defense. If the gun goes off at this point, it will be pointed at your attacker, and your problem will be solved. Anytime you can turn a weapon towards an attacker, or bring it close to them, you should, as this will create a problem for them to deal with, and turn them into the target.

Your right hand should move straight down, and behind your assailant's elbow (if you only manage to catch behind the wrist the technique will still work). It should now be brought up to join the hand that grabbed the gun, so that you have two hands on the weapon.

You can now rotate the gun, to put pressure on the wrist and force your assailant to release their grip. Once you have the gun in your hand, bring it forcibly back to strike your assailant's groin, then quickly move away from them.

Dealing with Weapon Retention

If your assailant pulls the gun back as you make your defense, you will have to follow their movement and stay close to them, so that you don't end up with the gun trained back on you.

Continue turning, and step forward with your right foot, so that you are now facing your assailant. The hand that initially moved downwards should now take an underhand grip on the gun. Both hands should now twist and turn the gun to point at your attacker—this will also force them to release their grip.

Rear Hostage with Arm Around Chest/Upper Body

If your assailant controls your upper body, as opposed to your neck, you will not be able to turn your body to move the gun into your attacker's face, and so you will have to focus on just moving it away from pointing at you. This isn't preferable, as it doesn't give your assailant any problems to deal with—i.e., putting them in the line of fire—and is biomechanically a weaker movement. Still, the situation needs to be solved.

Your right hand should turn quickly and grab the gun, pulling it forward to make your hand defense, while you move your head backwards (the body defense). The aim of both movements is to limit the amount of time that the gun is pointing at you.

Because of the position of the gun's barrel relative to your hand, you will not be able to use your thumb to grip, and will have to rely on your fingers alone to take hold of the weapon. Due to this disadvantage, you will need to get the second hand to the gun as quickly as possible.

If your assailant can control your upper body and prevent you from turning, you will need to make a different defense. (This technique is less preferable, as it moves the gun away from your attacker rather than towards them , and increases your chances of ending up back in the line of fire if your attacker pulls the gun back before you secure it.) Reach behind with the hand nearest the weapon and grab the gun. Note that you will not be able to grip using your thumb.

Pull the gun forward explosively (your hand defense), while throwing your head backwards (your body defense). Understand that because you are not able to close your thumb around the gun, your grip is relatively weak.

Position your other hand on the back of the gun where the hammer and rear sight are located, and continue to push the gun forwards.

Make sure that the gun is being pulled forwards and not downwards. Pulling the gun down will almost certainly mean that you end up pointing it at yourself.

Bend your knees and push your butt backwards as you pull the gun forwards. This will stretch out your assailant's arm and make it difficult for them to retain their weapon.

If you have extended your arm as far as you can and your assailant is still holding on to the gun, start to turn it outwards, away from you. This puts a great deal of pressure on their hand and will force them to release the weapon.

Keep turning the gun outwards, until they are no longer able to hold on to it.

Now slam the gun into your attackers's groin.

The second hand should assist the pulling action of the other hand by pushing at the back of the gun (roughly where the hammer is located).

As you make this movement, bend forward to pull the gun out of your attacker's reach, and push your butt back into them to move them back and fully extend their arm.

If they don't release because their arms are long enough to keep hold, twist the gun to your right to leverage it against their wrist to force a release.

Decision Making Under Stress

Under high levels of stress and emotion, where time is of the essence, you need to dispense with your normal decision-making processes, referred to as Rationalistic Decision Making (RDM). Normally when we deliberate to reach a decision, we evaluate each option and compare the pros and cons of each in order to work out what the best decision will be. This is a time-consuming process. In Naturalistic Decision Making (NDM), you don't look to choose the best option, you look to choose the very first effective solution available to you. If going for the gun to disarm your hostage taker is an effective solution, you should perform it—this will move you through the denial and deliberation loop, to a decision, and on to action.

If you can pre-build scripts that take you through this process, all to the better—e.g., "If an assailant moves me from one location to another, I will make a physical defense to prevent them," etc.

Knife Attacks

Knife attacks differ from threats in that your assailant has already decided to use their weapon—their intent to stab, cut, or slash is clear. The environment in which you are attacked will largely determine the way you handle an assault with a knife. If you have space to move, and obstacles and barriers you can put in front of your assailant, this should be your first approach to dealing with the situation. If you are attacked within a confined space, on the other hand, such as the bathroom of a bar or pub, your goal should be to restrict the movement of the blade— something which may end up seeing you get cut (particularly if the attack is frenzied, with your assailant making small, fast movements rather than long reaching, arcing slashes). In these close-range situations, you should also be prepared to deal with clothing grabs, head pulls and the like, which your attacker may attempt with their free hand.

It should be understood that the emotion and intent behind a stab is far more intense and serious than that behind a slash. For an untrained person, slashing tends to be wild and erratic, with the aim of cutting and maiming, rather than killing. When a person stabs, there is a definite intent to kill—this could be a subconscious intent rather than a conscious one, but the desire is the same. It may not have been their intent at the start of the fight, but when an assailant starts thrusting their knife, rather than swinging it, be aware of how they are now thinking.

Oftentimes when people are stabbed, they don't realize that a knife has been used, and they believe that they've been punched. They only realize what has happened to them when they see blood on their clothing. If you are in a crowded setting and suddenly "feel" impact to your body, buttocks, or legs—targets which are not that common on the street to attack with punches—you should immediately treat what is happening to you as a knife attack.

Rather than focus on a wide variety of knife attacks, many of which are very uncommon on the street (such as the straight stab), we will look at the two most common types of knife assaults: The oriental knife attack or "shank;" and rapid slashing cuts, which are extremely fast, small, and almost impossible to block.

The Oriental or "Shanking" Knife Attack

This attack has the ability to cause a serious amount of bodily trauma and injury, up to and including death, because the force behind the knife from the upwards swing is able to drive it a long way into the body. If the knife is being pulled out/recoiled with any circular or cycling motion, the blade will end up cutting in that fashion inside, meaning that the puncture wounds to internal organs will be much larger than if the knife had been driven in and pulled out in a straight line.

Somebody attacking in this fashion is a very serious and dangerous proposition, because they are in an emotional state where they are prepared to kill you. You either need to block and disengage, or take control of the attacking arm and incapacitate your attacker. If you simply disarm them, they will keep coming, and you may be overwhelmed before having a chance to use their knife against them (the only reason you would disarm them in the first place). It is much better to allow them to keep hold and focused on the knife as you use it against them.

360 Block with Strike and Disengagement

The body reacts naturally to any upwards motion coming towards the groin and midsection by sharply pulling the hips back. This natural response and movement will form the initial body defense, while your forearm coming down to aggressively attack the assailant's knife arm forms the hand defense. Because of the potential cycling of the knife, you need to be extremely aggressive in your blocking, so that your assailant's recoiling arm movement is seriously restricted. For your assailant, all thoughts of attack should be interrupted by the pain your blocking arm causes—that is your goal.

Come up on your toes so that you are deliberately off-balance (the fact that your hips are pulled back and your head is forward means that your stability has already been compromised), as you are going to exploit the fact that your body wants to fall forward to speed up your disengagement.

Your other hand should come straight up, in preparation for any second phase attack that your assailant may make. With your body in this position, with the hips back, you will not be able to make any power strikes; and should you decide to try to control the attacking arm, you will want your second hand to assist in this rather than use it to strike with.

Rather than step out, pull away your right foot and direct your weight so that you fall towards your attacker's left side; at the same time, push off explosively from your left foot. These two movements will mean that the transfer of weight needed for you to move will happen naturally, without any preliminary redistribution having to take place.

If you are engaged in a verbal dispute/conflict, be aware of what a person is carrying in their hand. Also watch their hands as you talk with them, so that you can see if they try to reach for a weapon. It is preferable to spoil somebody's draw and prevent a weapon from being pulled, to having to deal with it once it has been deployed.

It is important to understand that much of what happens in this sequence occurs due to the body's natural reflexes and responses. As the assailant swings the bottle/knife back, your body will anticipate the inevitable attack by starting to pull the hips and body away, and bringing the hands in to protect itself.

After pulling the hands in to protect, you will naturally push them out again to meet the attack. This is part of our natural "flinch" reflex—a response to fast movements that catch us by surprise. With training, you can educate this flinch response to result in a solid 360 Block, rather than the hands and arms being simply flung out in the hope of stopping the attack.

Your blocking arm should form a 90 degree angle at the elbow, as you want to stop the attack, not deflect it. Your other arm should be vertical, and lined up with your assailant's shoulder. This is there to protect you, should your assailant alter their attack, and swing their weapon upwards and inwards to your right side, aiming for your head.

Look to make impact with your assailant's weapon arm by slamming the blade of your forearm into it as hard as you can. If unchecked, your assailant will recoil their weapon and make multiple attacks. By changing the moment of impact by slamming your forearm into their attacking arm, you will interrupt the timing of their attacks.

Start to move offline, to your right. Your blocking arm should start to straighten and remain as a protective shield, guarding your left side. The forceful impact of your blocking arm should slow down their ability to make further attacks.

The blocking arm shouldn't move or deflect your assailant's weapon. It is simply straightened as you move to your right in order to offer a defensive barrier that can be used to prevent any further attacks. As you move, pull your right arm back, ready to make a strike.

As you move across, pull both hands back.

Move one hand (in this case, the right) to a position where a powerful strike can be made, and the other to a high guard position, which can protect the head.

With full force, turn the hips, and transfer your body weight forward to deliver a strong right punch to your assailant's jaw line. The strike should be thrown with everything you have, emotionally as well as physically—a punch backed by full emotion and aggression is much more powerful than a punch lacking these things.

Your arm should follow the body, staying at a 90 degree angle, with your forearm in a position to block and protect from any follow-up attack. As you move, you can use your right hand to rake the assailant's eyes, in order to disorient them.

360 Defense with Control

When disengagement isn't an option, either because your environment prevents you getting away from your assailant, or because there are people you don't want to leave behind, you will need to control the knife and then incapacitate your attacker. You will need to make the same initial 360 Block as you would to disengage. This time, rather than moving to the side, you are going to move in to control the arm holding the knife.

Your blocking motion should now turn into one where your hand is hooked behind your assailant's knife arm. Move in towards them, following and hopefully overtaking the movement of their recoiling arm. Your other hand should hook over the upper arm and assist by pulling you in towards your assailant. The wrist action of your left hand, coupled with the pull of your right, should result in your attacker's arm being rotated so that the knife is now pointed downwards—this isn't essential, but it makes further movement and control of the knife easier.

You should "hug" your assailant's arm close to your body, making sure that your left hand is clasping the wrist/lower forearm, rather than higher up the arm towards the elbow, where your aggressor may be able to get some bend in the arm and bring the knife back towards you. It also requires less strength to control a person at the wrist than at the elbow (if you can work with your whole body against the wrist, then you should have the strength and power advantage). If, when you block, you find yourself higher up the arm and away from the wrist, simply slide your grip down so that the focus is closer to the knife.

Now bring your right arm under your assailant's elbow, and take a grip with your left hand on your attacker's wrist. Push down with your left hand and pull in with your right. As you do this, slide your body around so that your assailant's knife hand is on your hips, with their forearm pinned tightly to your body. You can now push explosively upwards from the hip to drive your assailant's knife into their body.

To disengage, bring the knife up to your assailant's throat and then push them away.

When you are involved in an aggressive verbal altercation, try to create or maintain distance between yourself and your assailant. If they are holding a weapon, you will have to make an additional calculation to take its length into account.

As you instinctively anticipate the swing of the bottle/knife, your arms will naturally draw back to protect yourself. This happens before the arms are thrust out to meet whatever movement or attack has been detected.

This photo shows how the body naturally draws in the arms and pulls itself away from an attack...

...Before thrusting the arms out while continuing to pull the hips and body back. This is an instinctual movement, and one you will perform even when surprised and under duress. Our goal should be to train ourselves to work with these natural movements and build on them, to make better and more powerful defensive movements.

With the hips pulled back, drive the blade of your forearm into your assailant's attacking arm. This shock of pain should be unexpected by them, and so have a greater effect than anticipated pain, for which an assailant is prepared. Your goal is to cause a moment of hesitation, before they recoil their attack, in order to stab you again (attackers rarely rely on just a single attack).

Your body position should be with your head forward, your hips back, and in a slightly off-balanced position, with all of your weight wanting to fall forward. Go with this movement. There is little that will make you want to go towards a knife, and putting yourself in this position will force you to do so. Now "snake" your left arm under your assailant's attacking arm.

Use your right arm to help rotate your assailant's weapon arm, so that the bottle or knife is pointing downwards. The majority of this rotation is accomplished with your right wrist, which catches your assailant's wrist/ lower arm, and rotates it as you pull your hand to face you and in towards your chest.

You should end up clasping the attacker's weapon arm to your chest. It should be straight and pulled flush to you, there should be no space between your assailant's arm and your body. You should have an underhand grip with your left hand and an overhand grip with your right. Your left arm should be close to your attacker's weapon, and they should be pulled forward.

Keeping the arm tight to your chest, deliver a knee strike to your assailant's lower body. When you step back to place your foot back on the floor, pull your aggressor forward with you, to take their balance and keep them bending forward (the knee strike will have helped accomplish this).

Keeping a solid grip on your assailant's wrist, remove your top arm (right arm) and bring it up forcibly under your assailant's elbow joint.

As this makes impact and starts to bend their arm, start to move round to their right side.

Once you have control of the arm at the elbow joint, slide your left hand down to grip their weapon hand.

Continue turning to your attacker's side, and pull their weapon hand toward your hips.

Using your body, thrust the weapon into your attacker's side. You can do this repeatedly if necessary. At no point should your body and your assailant's arm lose contact.

Knife Shank with Pull From Behind

An assailant who shows you that they have a knife, or lets you see it, does so for a reason—they want to intimidate you and prepare themselves emotionally to use it, possibly because they want you to back away and run, or because they're not confident in making their assault unless they see that you are scared and unlikely to put up much of a fight.

An attacker who makes sure that you don't see their knife is someone who has only one goal in mind—to stab you. Stabbing from behind is perhaps the simplest and most direct way to ensure that you don't see the blade and don't have an opportunity to react and defend yourself. Rather than feeling like a knife stab, it may feel like a punch, so you must treat every attack from the rear that has the feeling of an "impact" as a potential knife attack.

This type of assault may occur after you have been in some form of altercation or verbal dispute, which you may believe has been resolved. It may be that you knocked into somebody in a bar, apologized, and thought the whole affair was over (after offering to buy them a drink and pay for their dry cleaning, etc.), not realizing that the friends of the person you bumped into have told him he should have done something, rather than accepting your apology. After a few more drinks and some more verbal abuse from his friends, he sees you walk into the bathroom and decides to follow you. At this point he may not have any "formal" plan in his mind, but he knows he has to save face in front of his friends and show them that he's capable of sticking up for himself. As he walks behind you, he becomes more emotionally charged, as he relives the jeers, taunts, and abuse his friends gave him. As he becomes more enraged, he feels the knife (which he carries for self defense) pressing against him in his pocket, and pulls it out/open. Grabbing your right shoulder with his left hand, he pulls you back, making an oriental stab with his right hand.

As you are pulled backwards, your hands will start to come up naturally. At this point, you won't know whether the attack will be high, such as a punch to the head, or low, such as a stab to the buttocks or back (or even to the stomach, if the aim of your assailant's pull is to turn you around). This means you will have to make two defenses at once, and follow up whichever one ends up intercepting the attack. If there is no attack combined with the pull—as if somebody is simply violently pulling you back—then your defense should be able to be used as your own attack, to disrupt any further assault on their part.

As you are pulled backwards, turn and take a step (with your right leg), going with the movement of the pull. If you try to resist the pull, all your energy and effort will be spent dealing with the pulling action, which in itself isn't putting you in much danger. It is the attack with the second hand that is the real threat. As you do this, swing your right arm up and around towards where you anticipate your attacker's head and neck to be. The arm should be straight—if your assailant is following up with a punch, you need to get your forearm to meet their attacking arm as soon as possible, and if the arm is bent at the elbow, your arm may take too long to intercept the strike. If there is no punch, or similar high attack, your fist or forearm should impact onto your assailant's head or neck.

As you make this block or strike, raise your shoulder up out of the socket as you turn so it comes close to your neck. If your assailant is choking you or has grabbed your neck in any way, this motion will help break their grip.

Your left hand should come low and form a 360 Block. This may be a redundant action if the attack is a pull followed by a punch or other similarly high attack. However, when you are pulled from behind, you have no idea what form the attack might take, and without this block you could end up being fatally stabbed. If you feel impact on your low blocking arm, you know that you are in all likelihood dealing with a knife, and you should execute a control.

There is a big difference between an assailant who shows you a weapon and one that keeps it hidden and out of sight. An assailant who shows you a weapon does so to intimidate you, maybe as part of a threat to get you to acquiesce to a demand, or because they are not emotionally ready to use it yet. If it is the latter, you should act preemptively.

An assailant who keeps their weapon hidden is another proposition. This individual doesn't want to give you any warning that they are about to stab or cut you. You should be very suspicious of anyone whose hands are out of sight, or placed around their pockets or belt area. In such situations, try to bring your hand to the level of their hands so you only have to move your hands in one plane/direction to gain control of the knife.

Group dynamics can force reluctant individuals to engage in conflicts that they would otherwise ignore and/or walk away from. Through peer pressure, an individual may feel forced to right a perceived wrong, such as having a drink accidentally spilt over them. People become violent when they feel justified to do so and see no other alternatives.

Imagine a situation where you accidentally spilt somebody's drink over them. In your mind it was sorted out when you brought them another drink and/or gave them money for dry cleaning. However, after a few drinks, and under constant pressure from their friends, the individual feels that to preserve their status in the group they need to punish you physically.

As you make your way to the bathroom, you are pulled violently from behind. At this point you don't know whether you are simply being pulled, or are about to be punched or stabbed. You need to perform a defensive counter that deals with all of these possibilities.

Do not waste time fighting against the pulling motion, but turn and go with it, closing the distance between you and your attacker. One arm should look to make a high block (or strike), and the other hand should be positioned to block anything that may be coming in low.

The high arm does one of two things: it can be used to block a strike if your assailant has pulled you onto a punch, or it can be used to make a forearm strike to the neck, if there is no high attack. The other arm comes out at a 90 degree angle to block any low strikes, such as in a shanking motion.

In this case, the attack is via a low shank, so the bottom arm blocks this movement, and the forearm is slammed into your assailant's neck.

At this point, you should have caused serious trauma to your assailant's neck, and stopped the low armed attack.

"Snake" your blocking arm under your assailant's weapon arm and pull it to your chest. The arm that made the forearm strike to the neck should be used to rotate your assailant's weapon arm, so that the knife/ bottle is pointing down.

Pull your assailant's arm to your chest, so that their arm is trapped flush against it. At this point, you can throw a knee strike, if necessary.

Remove your top arm and strike upwards at your attacker's elbow joint, while keeping a solid control with the other arm.

Move to your attacker's side and slide your left hand down to control the attacker's weapon hand at your hips.

Using your body/hips, drive upwards into your assailant, stabbing them with the weapon. As soon as you can, exit the situation, as you want to avoid a situation where your assailant's friends get involved.

Knife Shank with Clothing Grab

Over the course of this interaction, the aggressor has become more emotionally charged and is ready to make a more committed, extreme, and violent assault. The solution in such a situation is to immediately attempt to disengage or attack with full force at the first push or grab, with the aim of incapacitating your aggressor and ending the fight quickly. If this is not done, you leave room for your assailant to become more aggressive, while also giving them the motivation and opportunity to make a more extreme assault, such as grabbing your lapels and attempting to shank you.

In this scenario, your assailant grabs your clothing to make sure that you cannot back away from their knife shank. Your problem here is that their grabbing arm will prevent you from moving in to control the knife arm, as they will simply be able to stiffen the arm and push you away. Your first instinct will be to defend the knife shank, and you will do this with a downwards 360 Block (making a hand-defense with your forearm, and a body defense by pulling the hips back—both are natural responses to the upwards motion of the blade). Your right hand should now shoot up to grab the hand that is holding your lapel.

Notice how similar the body movement is to the normal Oriental Knife Attack defense (see pages 133–134), where the right hand comes up to block potential second phase assaults—and/or in the case of a control, is ready to grab the assailant's upper arm.

As the knife recoils for the next attack, drag your left foot back in a circular fashion. With the arm that has control of your assailant's weapon arm, bring the elbow up. This should rotate their wrist and arm, so that the arm is now locked out straight. By locking the arm and pulling your body back, you have created an obstacle between you and your assailant's knife (if you can rip the grip free at this point and disengage to get a weapon, you should). At the same time, you have managed to create distance. As all of this is happening, your blocking hand should come up and grab your attacker's wrist, assisting your first hand. Now you can drop the right elbow down, so that both hands are over your attacker's wrist, with your thumbs underneath. You are now in a position to apply a wrist lock.

For this to work, you must ensure that the grip on your assailant's hand/wrist will allow the wrist to still move. The wrist has very little lateral movement, so this lock/control should come on very quickly. Using your body to lean into their hand/fist, pull down with your pinkies and push up with your thumbs. This will bring your aggressor to their knees. Now pull them towards you, keeping their wrist pressed to your chest, until they are face down on the ground. Now either disengage, or use stomp kicks to the arms, legs, and body—and even the head (if the situation is life-threatening).

An attacker may grab you as part of an oriental/shank attack. This will prevent you from disengaging, striking, and/or controlling the weapon arm. This is an occasion where although the knife/bottle attack has to be dealt with, your focus should be on controlling your assailant via their grabbing arm.

As the attack comes in, you will naturally bring your arms in to protect yourself.

Your arm closest to the grabbing arm should come up and grab the hand that is holding your shirt (you must grab the hand itself). The other hand should drive outwards to make a protective 360 Block against the bottle/knife.

Your hips should be back, your block should have impacted with the weapon arm, and you should have hold of your assailant's grabbing hand (the elbow should be down with the hand gripping from below).

As soon as the block has been made and the recoil of the bottle/knife begins, bring your other hand up to grab your attacker's hand in a similar grip as your first hand.

Begin to step back with your left leg, away from the knife/bottle, straightening your attacker's arm.

Start to bring your right elbow upwards, rotating your assailant's arm. You want to end up in a position where their little finger is pointing upwards and the wrist can move freely. If you need to reposition your hands to do this, i.e., bring your elbows back down, this is the time to do it. Keep your assailant's hand locked to your body.

Using your body to put pressure on their wrist, lean into your attacker's arm. At the same time, push you hands upwards to bend their wrist, and then drive down. (To get an idea of how the lock works, hold your arm straight out to your side, parallel with the floor, and then rotate it so your little finger is pointing upwards. Now bend the wrist to point your little finger towards the sky.)

Keep driving down as you pull your assailant forward. The wrist doesn't have much movement/flexibility in the direction you are bending it (your hands must grab your attacker's hand in order for the wrist to move freely), and the lock/control should come on quickly.

Keep dragging your assailant down until they are flat on the ground. From here you should look to disengage, and/or find a weapon to use if disengagement isn't an option.

Maybe you are in a situation where you are involved in a verbal altercation with someone, who has overcome their reluctance to use force but has not yet reached the stage where they're emotionally charged enough to punch or hit you. This is a common ritual that people go through, using pushes, shoves, and clothing grabs to try to demonstrate their physical dominance over you, test your response to their actions, and generally work themselves up into a state of anger where they are ready to cause serious damage. As soon as somebody touches you, it is an assault. In most cases you should respond to this with physical force, as (by this point) the time for talking has passed.

Most fights start with a verbal confrontation, followed by some show of force. Many individuals try to avoid fighting by posturing and trying to intimidate the person they are dealing with, e.g., they may push you to demonstrate that they are able to handle themselves and that you shouldn't mess with them. This is the time to either walk away or attack.

Unfortunately, many people choose to respond with equal force, rather than walking away.

If you push your assailant in response, the conflict has no possibility of ending because neither person will walk away or make a decisive assault on the other, but instead carry on escalating the situation.

Rather than pushing back, you should have either attacked decisively, or walked away.

In this situation, the person who was initially pushed simply pushed back, upping the ante. The original aggressor cannot simply push again, but must escalate their use of force, to demonstrate their dominance. We refer to this as a "Monkey Dance"—an escalating show of force without anyone actually taking decisive action.

Now the aggressor launches an actual attack. The person who was originally pushed missed their opportunity to preempt the fight; they merely postured back, rather than launching an all out assault against their aggressor the moment they pushed them. If somebody touches you in an aggressive manner, either disengage or attack—don't just up the ante.

What often happens when one person starts pushing is that the other person pushes back, as each tries to show that they quite literally can't be pushed around. Gradually, things start to get more violent, with slaps, pushes to the face and neck, etc., until one person throws a punch or pulls a weapon. This gradual "upping the ante" is a mistake that many people make, believing that if they can just show that they're not a victim, their aggressor will back down. They don't realize that by taking this approach, they are actually demonstrating that they are also a threat to their assailant, and therefore somebody who must now be dealt with.

Knife Shank with Clothing Grab Against a Wall

It would be naive to think that an attacker will always grant you the space in which to make an adequate defense. An assailant will often use the surrounding environment to help facilitate their assault. A committed attacker armed with a knife will want to deny you any space which might allow you to move away from the knife (make a body defense). One way they may do this is to drive you into a wall, car, or other object that will prevent you from moving or escaping the attack.

In this situation, an aggressor has followed you into the bathroom. They are going to use the environment to restrict your movement and your ability to defend and respond to their attack.

As you turn away from the sink, your assailant grabs you and starts to push you into the wall, as they stab upwards towards you with a knife.

With your back to the wall, it will be difficult for you to make a body defense by pulling the hips back. This means you will have to bend forward more and come to meet the knife, not just with your arm, but with your body as well. Instead of grabbing over the weapon arm with your right arm, grab under it behind the elbow.

Pull at the elbow and push at the wrist to straighten their arm.

At the same time, start to "snake" the hand on the wrist round so you can pull the attacker's weapon arm towards you.

You should be controlling the arm with two underhand grips and have the weapon arm flush against your chest.

Using the arm as a lever, ram/drive your attacker into the wall. At any point in a conflict where you can use the environment to your advantage, you should do so, whether it be the ground, a wall, the corner of a table, etc. These are all good striking surfaces to use.

Now transfer the hand nearest to the weapon to control the weapon hand itself.

Keeping a good grip on the weapon arm, turn your attacker's knife toward them.

Now move round to the side.

Use your hips to drive the knife into the attacker's body.

With your back against a wall, you will be unable to move away from the knife (and have the space to control the arm that is controlling your clothing and movement). At the same time, you don't have to worry about being put off-balance, because the wall will help stabilize your movement.

Your first defense is to make a 360 Block/Defense against the knife attack, with the addition of your other hand shooting past your blocking hand to control the knife as the attacker recoils the weapon. Control the arm above the elbow.

Immediately lock the arm straight and pull your assailant towards you, then move to the side, using the arm that shot through (the right, in this scenario) to help pull your assailant towards the wall. Step away to allow them to hit the wall with force—this is how you use the environment to your advantage. Keep moving until you are at your assailant's side and then slip your arm through to press the forearm against your chest and transfer your hand to grab the knife. You can explode with your hips and stab them in the side.

Fast Slashing Movements that are too Small to Block

Sometimes, the knife moves so fast that it is impossible to block it with the hands. In fact, trying to get an arm in to block a fast-moving knife would be the equivalent of putting your hand into a food processor, as the knife movements are so small and so fast. Although 360 Blocks work well against an assailant who moves their arm outside of their silhouette, when the attacks are very small, such blocks are almost impossible to make.

To deal with this type of attack, step back away from the slashes and drop to the ground (in a low crouch/squat), pulling your feet under you. This should put you below the knife. Immediately explode forward, keeping as close to the ground as you can. Hit the front of your assailant's ankle with your shoulder, while swinging the arm round to trap their leg from behind. You can now drive forward to take their balance and force them to ground. Now disengage and find a weapon of your own.

When an assailant makes large, slashing movements where the knife passes outside of their body shape, you can use regular 360 defenses to block.

When the slashing motions are small and fast, with the knife moving inside the attacker's shape/silhouette, it is virtually impossible to make an effective 360 Block—it would be like putting your hand into a food processor to try to stop the blades.

If an attacker's knife slashes are too fast and small for you to make an effective block, you must forget about trying to block the knife and find a way of disabling your attacker. If there are no barriers/obstacles to get behind and nothing you can use as an improvised weapon, you should move away from your attacker, timing your footwork...

...So that you can drop under the knife. This technique is not without its risks. However, it has the effect of catching your attacker off-guard, and forces them to consider how they must now change their attack in order to deal with you. Ideally, you should time your drop to coincide with your attacker committing their weight to their forward leg.

You need to drop incredibly low, and keep your face towards the floor. Even if your assailant is able to react and bring their slashes down towards you, they will not be able to do much damage without changing their grip so that the blade is pointing down towards you where it can be used to stab rather than slash.

Keeping low to the ground, drive forwards, catching your assailant's forward leg. If they have committed their weight to it, they will have great difficulty pulling the leg back.

With your arm behind their ankle, drive forward with your shoulder, forcing them to ground.

Most people's natural response when they fall is to let go of what they are holding in order to use their arms/hands to break their fall. Your assailant may be able to cut you if they still hold on to the knife, but their falling will prevent them from doing so effectively. They certainly won't have time to change the knife position so they can stab downwards.

Keep driving forward until they are flat on the floor.

As you stand up, grab the same leg you used to take them down.

Lift the leg up...

...And throw it away from you, so that your assailant is on their side/front and no longer facing you.

Stamp down hard on their ankle, so they will be unable to get up and continue the fight.

Now disengage. There may be third parties in the environment who are able to come to your attacker's assistance.

Control of the Environment—Improvised Weapons and Obstacles

Never deal with a knife from an "empty hands" position, if you have the option of using a weapon to improve your odds. You should similarly use the terrain and objects in it to provide obstacles to put between yourself and your assailant. These strategies should be defaulted to without hesitation.

In outdoor settings, cars can make excellent barriers to put both distance and a "shield" between you and a knife-wielding assailant. Many people will fall into the trap of thinking that unless you disarm or disable your attacker, you will have lost the fight. Often, it is enough to simply prevent your assailant from doing what they want to do to you, and disengagement, coupled with a barrier, can accomplish this. If an aggressor is unable to complete their assault within a brief time, they may start to lose their emotional commitment to harm you—especially if they are no longer adrenalized (and this state only lasts for 10–15 seconds). If you are able to buy time and put a seed of doubt in their mind about their ability to harm you, they may become convinced that violence is not an option for them (at this time). Using your environment to facilitate your survival is a key self-defense skill.

Using a table as a barrier can create the time for you to get to a personal carry weapon like CS spray in this situation, and the range/ distance for you to successfully deploy it. If you do carry a weapon for personal protection you should have an understanding of previolence indicators that would prompt you to deploy it, and train to create the distance from an aggressor to make this possible.

A car makes a perfect obstacle/barrier to put between you and an assailant. It is not always necessary to physically destroy an attacker—sometimes, it is enough to simply prevent them from doing what they want to do to you. If an attacker can't get to you, they can't attack you.

Improvised Weapons

Barriers and obstacles can also be used to create enough time and distance to retrieve your own weapon, if you carry one (such as CS spray, a baton, a sidearm, etc.), or to recognize and find an object that could be used as an improvised weapon. Many people see improvised weapons as a quick fix, or even a starting point of self-defense. I actually see it as the pinnacle of combat training. If you can understand how to make a tool out of something found in your environment, then you have an exceptional mind—you are going back to the basic instincts and ideas that first enabled man to discover fire, create the wheel, etc. Improvised weapons are the height of invention, and necessity is the mother of invention. If in a moment you can create a "tool" while under emotional pressure, then you are at your most human, doing what human beings do best.

Many people confuse improvised weapons as fighting using everyday objects—such as pens, belts, chairs, etc. If you have been trained to look for a chair, and have trained in how to use it as a weapon, then you are not "improvising," you are using an everyday object which you have specifically trained to use. There is nothing wrong with this, but you would need to train with a lot of different objects in order to have a comprehensive system of self-defense. If you are able to improvise, however, you will be able to recognize the potential in every object you see. In learning to improvise a weapon, you should take some time in your daily routine to categorize objects you see around you in the following way:

- Stick-like objects
- Shield-like objects
- Knife-like objects
- Chain/flexible objects
- Rock/stone objects
- Small objects

A chair can be used as a shield to keep distance between you and an attacker, as well as block any attacks they make. You can also use it as a weapon, utilizing its legs as sticks. Hold the chair "diagonally," lining up one leg with your attacker's groin and the opposite one with their face. You can now jab the legs towards these two targets.

When using any weapon, but especially an improvised one, you should be aware of its limitations and restrictions. For example, a fire extinguisher can make a great shield-like weapon, which can also cause great trauma if used as an impact weapon, but it can also be fairly heavy and unwieldy, depending on its size.

Keys on a key chain slashed at somebody's face can work well, but only against exposed skin; similar to small objects, such as coins that can be thrown.

A rolled up magazine has many stick-like properties, and can generate great force when used for stabbing. It is not so effective when used to strike in a swiping motion, however.

As well as being used in a chain-like fashion, keys can be used to cut like a knife when held statically—don't put them between your fingers like a knuckle-duster, but hold one between your thumb and finger like a small knife. Remember that the range needed to use them in this fashion will bring you in to close proximity with your assailant, as would using a can or water bottle as an impact tool. These are the things that you must intrinsically understand about the tool you identify as the most suitable to use in the situation you are dealing with.

You can also combine various objects, e.g., a pile of quarters in a condom makes a good chain-like weapon. If you are in a club/bar and you believe there is the potential threat of violence, with little or no chance of disengaging from the situation, going to the bathroom and constructing such a weapon may be a good survival option. However, for most improvised weapons to be useful, they should be at hand and require little or no construction/alteration in order for them to be used.

Attempting to fight empty-handed against an assailant armed with a knife (or even unarmed for that matter, as you should assume they're armed, technically skilled, and with others in the environment who will come to their assistance) should be a last resort, not a first choice. When somebody comes at you with a blade, they will have put themselves in a certain emotional place and will be in a highly volatile state. Their ability to reason and contemplate the consequences of their actions will have left them, and they will have only one goal in mind—to seriously hurt, injure, or even kill you. There is a lot to equalize in such a situation, and using a weapon (either improvised or otherwise) should be a "go to" strategy—a first choice.

PART 3

Unarmed Assaults and Dynamic Components of Violence

Introduction

The most common assaults you are likely to face involve being pushed, pulled, or punched. It is very hard for somebody to initiate a fight with a front headlock/guillotine or side headlock, etc. These are things that happen in the midst of a fight, and it is important to understand that with good movement, control of range, and accurate striking, you can prevent these things from happening to you.

Unarmed assaults from the rear, however, are a means by which an assailant can initiate an assault without first engaging in some form of pushing, pulling, or striking.

Rear Strangle

Attacks from the rear are probably not the most common ones that you will face—however, they are the ones we fear the most, as they give us the least time to prepare, and are committed by assailants who are not looking for any alternative to violence. These attacks may be committed by a single assailant, or they may occur in multiple attacker scenarios, where you are dealing (either verbally or physically) with an aggressor to the front when you are attacked by their friend or accomplice from the rear. By moving and scanning with your eyes as you deal with an assailant, you can avoid this happening.

You may be involved in a multiple attacker situation where both assailants come up behind you. Maybe you were involved in some small verbal altercation in a bar or club, which happened early enough in the evening that you have forgotten all about it. As you walk home (or to your car), you feel the hairs on the back of your neck stand up and you recognize the sound of footsteps several feet behind you. Your initial reaction is one of fear, but you immediately tell yourself that you are being stupid and only imagining the danger. This is a natural response to a threat, and is part of the Denial, Deliberation, Decision, and Action Continuum that almost every untrained individual follows (see page 107). Your best response would be to turn around immediately and assess the threat. However, as you are thinking about doing this, your assailants close the distance and you feel yourself being pulled back.

As you try to regain balance, your hands will automatically come up to try to clear the attack on your windpipe that is depriving your lungs of air. You don't have to think about making this defense, your body will do it automatically. (This is one of the great strengths of Krav Maga—the utilization of the body's natural responses.) If you accompany this movement by turning your head to the side and looking at your assailant, you will alleviate some of the pressure on your throat.

At the moment, your assailant will be controlling your movement, which will make it hard for you to make any appropriate defense, and so you will need to regain your balance and start to push them back, rather than allowing them to pull you. Drive the back of your head into their shoulder and start forcibly running backwards into them. This will firstly, turn you into the attacker and your aggressor into the victim—an important mental shift for you both; secondly, allow you to get your feet back under you, so you can make an effective escape; and thirdly, make you a harder target for any second assailant to attack, as you are dictating the movement of the fight.

As you move back, take your left foot and step behind your primary assailant. As you do this, explosively pluck down on your attacker's arm, utilizing your back muscles, and drop your weight to focus everything on clearing the arm that is obstructing your airways. In Krav Maga there is a principle, "If it's a life threatening attack, attack the attack; if it's a non-life threatening attack, then attack the attacker."

At the moment, you are dealing with a life-threatening attack—if you can't breathe, you will quickly lose consciousness, so all of your efforts should be focused on dealing with the arm that is strangling you. Once you have moved the arm away from your throat, secure the assailant's forearm against your chest, pulling it into you. This will prevent it from re-tightening on your throat.

As you step back, make sure that you keep your chin tucked in, with your face to the side—the position you first adopted as a defense against the strangulation—as this will stop your chin acting as a hook that could get caught on your attacker's forearm and lead to you potentially getting caught in a Side Headlock. As you create the space to pull your head out, keep pulling on the assailant's arm so it is straight, then roll your right shoulder over their arm just above the elbow joint (you should still be holding on to their arm, pressing it into your body). With the elbow isolated, drop your right shoulder and pull up with your left arm to hyperextend the elbow joint.

As you are walking towards your car, you fail to notice an individual who has synchronized their movement to yours.

Without warning, they try to strangle you, dragging you backwards. Instinctively, your hands come up to try to protect your throat and clear your airway. This is a natural movement that you will do automatically. To deal with this, press the back of your head into your attacker, and use them to help support you, then drive them backwards.

While you drive them backwards—you are pushing them, rather than being pulled—turn your head inwards. This will help relieve the pressure against your throat, and also stop your chin getting caught on the assailant's forearm when you eventually make an escape. You should now start to explosively pull down on your attacker's arm.

Continue to pull down, using your back rather than arm muscles, stepping behind your attacker as you drop with your weight.

As you step through and under their arm, lift your shoulder up so that you don't bend over too much.

As you step out of the hold/control, pull your assailant's arm, and roll your shoulder over their elbow joint, pulling upwards on the wrist to hyperextend their arm.

Now move towards the assailant, driving into them.

Push them away before disengaging. Do not be overly concerned with getting to your car—your goal should be to get to a most quickly accessible safe place, not necessarily the nearest. It may be faster for you to run back to the building where you came from, rather than trying to retrieve your car keys and unlock the car. You can always call the police and return to your car with them later.

If you want to have greater control of your attacker, after hyperextending their arm, you can thread the hand/arm that was nearest to the wrist through the arm they used to strangle you with, to put pressure on the elbow joint. You should not look on this as an arm lock, but more as a way of putting them in a more disadvantageous position.

Now shove them away.

Applying an Effective Rear Strangle

There may well be times when you find yourself behind an attacker and in a position to apply your own rear strangle/attack. To properly and effectively strangle somebody, you need to do more than simply pull your forearm back into your assailant's throat.

First, you need to ensure that the boniest part of your forearm—your wrist—is the part that is pressed into your attacker's throat. You should join both hands together (your left hand may well have been used to push on the base of your assailant's spine to put them off balance—this also helps equalize differences in height) and rather than pull straight back, rotate your right hand so the thumb comes up and the pinky/little finger points down. At the same time, push your right shoulder into the back of their head, so that the spine becomes hyperextended at the neck. The combination of your wrist cutting in, and your shoulder driving against the back of the head and throat, will crush and constrict their windpipe.

To apply an effective rear strangle, get behind your assailant and slide your wrist and forearm tightly across their neck. You should aim to get the bony part of your wrist across their windpipe. Position your shoulder behind their head. Drive forward with your shoulder, while "scooping" your wrist inwards and upwards. You can talk to them as you do this.

Dynamic Factors within a Fight

A fight is a dynamic thing that contains many dimensions (striking, grappling, ground, weapons, etc.). A knife is as likely to be pulled in the middle of a fight as it is at the beginning; just as you think you are controlling range and movement with your striking, you can lose your footing; or suddenly find your attacker trying to pull you forward into a clinch. Below are some examples of attacks you may get caught up in. That is not to say an attacker won't initiate an assault with one of the attacks listed, but rather they are more likely to occur after the first attack has already been made.

Front Headlock/Guillotine

You become vulnerable to a Front Headlock when your head passes forward past your hips (this is one reason it's important to keep your head directly over your hips, and stay upright). This may happen because you have wound up inadvertently ducking to avoid being punched, or leaning forward when throwing a punch of your own. These are both common mistakes. It can also happen when a skilled assailant closes the distance effectively because they intend to make such an attack.

Every attack has a movement that is the focus of the attack, and one that is the source of its power. The Front Headlock/Guillotine is a good example of this, with the power provided by the blade of the forearm against the throat (the focus of the attack) and the hips pushing forward and lifting up the neck. To make an effective and complete defense, both parts of the attack must be neutralized.

Preventing a Front Headlock

As your head is pulled down, step forward with the movement—don't fight this, but go with it. You should never fight against somebody's pull, but instead add to the movement. As you make the step, bring your biceps close to your ears, so that if your assailant tries to move their arm to choke you, your arms will protect your neck—where the focus of the attack will be.

Put your hands on your attacker's hips and explosively push them backwards, taking the power away from their hips. Make sure that you move your assailant backwards, rather than pushing yourself backwards off of them.

Immediately follow up with punches, kicks, etc. It is important to take the power of your attacker's hips away, as often when your head is being pulled down it is hard to tell if the attack you are dealing with is a front headlock or a knee strike. By pushing the hips back, you deal with either one. With the arms out in front of you for the push, you will be able to turn this into an effective block if a knee strike does come in.

If you are able to control the range and distance of a fight, you should be able to avoid being strangled, locked, held, clinched, or choked. However, there are times when these things do happen, and you must be prepared to deal with them. In this instance, an attacker manages to grab your head and starts to pull you down to apply a guillotine choke/front headlock.

As the assailant pulls you down, follow their movement and step towards them, placing your hands on their hips. In the photo you can see the attacker trying to bring his right arm around, to put the forearm across your throat (and choke you out).

By keeping your upper arms by your ears, you are able to protect your neck/throat. Your attacker may be able to get their arm across your neck, but they will have also caught both of your arms, and so won't be able to apply a choke.

Start to push on your attacker's hips, driving them backwards. For the front headlock/guillotine choke to be effective, they would have to drive their hips forward once they had their forearm across your throat, in order to apply pressure. Even if they had managed to get their forearm across your throat at this stage, pushing their hips back would stop them applying the choke.

Once you have pushed them away, immediately attack them with strikes, punches, elbows, knees, etc. Although you have prevented them from applying a choke/lock, until you begin to damage them you have done nothing to stop them from continuing the assault. While their hips are back and out of position, they are vulnerable to your attack.

The Single Wing Clothing Choke

Whenever you find yourself in a position where you are behind or to the side of your attacker, with one arm under one of their arms, you will be able to apply a Single Wing Clothing Choke. There are a variety of ways you can end up in this position, three of which are listed below:

1. Escaping from a clinch
2. Defending a push
3. Escaping a guillotine choke

After you break free from the guillotine choke, you should be able to position yourself so that your right hand hooks under your assailant's right arm. From here, step behind your attacker and grab either their right collar, or a good handful of their clothing, and pull it across and around their neck.

After escaping a guillotine choke/front headlock...

...Step under your assailant's arm, delivering a groin strike with your right hand.

Step behind your assailant, bringing your left hand around their neck, and your right hand under their right arm.

Your left arm should reach round and grab their t-shirt, shirt, or jacket somewhere around their right shoulder/upper lapel area.

Your right hand, which is under your attacker's right arm, should shoot up and slide behind their neck.

Start to pull your assailant's t-shirt/clothing around their neck, while sliding your other arm behind your attacker's neck and under your left wrist. Both arms will be bent at this stage.

Step back and straighten your arms. This will pull the material around your attacker's neck, restricting blood flow to the carotid processes (these regulate blood pressure in the head and when they stop receiving blood, they interpret this to signify the head/brain is overloaded with blood and so will flush it, while lowering the heart rate at the same time). Unconsciousness will soon follow.

This close-up shows the final hand position. The left hand is pulling the material around the neck, while the right arm is pushing against the back of the neck.

Raise your right hand up and slide it behind your attacker's neck, under the wrist of your left arm. At this point, both of your elbows will be bent to apply the choke.

Straighten your arms by stepping back slightly. Straightening the arms will pull the material of your assailant's clothing around their neck, restricting blood flow to the carotid arteries and the carotid processes, thereby fooling the body into thinking there is excess blood pressure in the brain. This will cause the body to prevent more oxygenated blood from being pumped to the brain, resulting in the person being rendered unconscious.

One of the great benefits of chokes and strangulations is that every person, regardless of size or strength, is vulnerable to them—they provide an automatic shut-off. It doesn't matter how many hours a person spends in the gym, how big or strong they are, or how high their pain tolerance is (due to natural or artificial means, as with alcohol or drug use)—you can still be choked out with the same effort that it takes to choke someone who weighs 120 lbs (55 kg).

When the Front Choke has been Applied

If your assailant manages to get a choke on, and their forearm starts to dig into your windpipe, restricting the flow of oxygen to your lungs as with the rear strangle, your hands will instinctively reach up to try to claw it away. In such an instance, your head will be trapped under your assailant's armpit and you won't have room to turn your head to the side to protect it.

Once your hands reach the attacking arm, explosively pull down— you can add power to your attack by bending the knees and jumping slightly, so your attacker's arm is being pulled down by your entire bodyweight (it is unnecessary to exaggerate this jump, as all you require is a small, sharp drop in weight). Use your larger back muscles as you quickly pluck down, rather than simply trying to pull with the arms.

As soon as you have the space, turn your face to the side, while "rolling" your shoulder over your attacker's arm(s), so that if they tried to reapply the choke, they would be pulling against your shoulder and upper chest, rather than against your throat.

Once your neck is safe (and you have dealt with the life-threatening component of the assault), start attacking your assailant with slaps to the groin. This will cause their hips to move back as they react to the strikes, and will bring their head forward. Explosively pull the elbow back and up, with the aim of landing a solid strike to their face.

To escape the hold, step through to a position where you can apply the Single Wing Clothing Choke. To do this, you should pull down with your left hand, while explosively moving your right hand up, attacking your assailant's wrist with the blade of your forearm.

Now step through and behind your aggressor, while raising your right arm up to trap the arm that was applying the choke. Reach around and grab the right collar of your attacker. Follow this up by sliding your right arm under your left wrist—at this point your elbows will be bent. Now straighten the arms, by stepping back—it should feel as if both wrists are a pivot point for your arms—and the choke will be applied.

If you have been unsuccessful in preventing the guillotine choke, your attacker will have their forearm across your throat and be attacking your airway. This will cause you to instinctively bring up your hands to free your neck. This is a life-threatening attack and so you should attack the attack, not the attacker.

If the attacker has managed to drive their hips forward, you will probably be up on your toes. Drop your weight, pulling your feet under you, and explosively pluck down with your arms, utilizing your larger back muscles. Immediately roll your shoulder over your attacker's arms, so they are now across your upper body, not your neck.

Keeping hold of your attacker's right arm, and maintaining your body position, release your left hand and start striking their groin. At this point your assailant may release the hold, allowing you to escape.

If you can't escape, raise your elbow to strike your attacker's face.

Then swing your arm forwards and upwards...

...Cutting through your attacker's hands where they grip together. Your right hand should assist by explosively pulling down at the same time.

Immediately step through to escape, forcing your right shoulder through the gap, so your assailant can't reapply the hold.

Applying an Effective Guillotine

The guillotine can be an effective attacking option as well—especially if your assailant drops their head forward or covers up from your strikes. The reason you were able to make an effective defense against this attack is because your attacker was controlling your head, but was not able to control or nullify the power of your hips, meaning that they didn't have total control of your body (for a person to fully control you, they must control both your head and hips, otherwise you'll be able to move one or the other to escape).

To take the hips out of play (rather than just put your attacker's head under your armpit), you are going to use the side of your thumb and the edge of your forearm to rotate your attacker's head so that you have it controlled partly under your armpit and partly under your chest. This action rotates the spine, hyperextends the neck, and takes the hips out of alignment (one of your assailant's feet may well be off the ground, or at least in a position where they're not able to put any significant weight on it). Once the head is in this position, you can move your forearm across their windpipe.

To apply the choke itself, put your left hand on your attacker's right trapezius muscle/upper back, and put your right hand on your left wrist. Push your hips forward, and bring your elbows together.

The guillotine choke can be a very effective way to finish a fight. However, there are different ways it can be applied, some more effective than others. One problem many people have is that when choking a person who is taller, it is not possible to get enough pressure on their neck/throat, as they simply stand taller than you when you drive your hips through.

By not placing the head so far under your armpit and twisting it in a way that takes the spine out of alignment, an individual can't take pressure off their throat by simply standing taller. To fully apply this type of choke, bring both of your elbows towards each other and drive up with the hips.

As well as applying a choke whose pressure is almost impossible to relieve, you have an effective neck crank as well. If you wanted to apply serious trauma to the neck, simply dropping to sit down under your attacker would see them thrown over you, with all their weight being directed into their neck and spine.

Another advantage of applying a guillotine choke this way is that it will allow you to choke people who are significantly taller than you. If you don't rotate the spine and take the hips out of line, a much taller assailant will simply be able to stand up when you attack with a conventional guillotine, thus protecting their airway. By already turning the head, you prevent your assailant from doing this (as seen in the previously detailed defense against a guillotine).

Fighting from a Clinch

A fight is a messy and scrappy affair. Everything will happen much faster than you think, and although it will usually end quickly, the whole event, when you think back to it, will feel like it lasted an eternity (contrary to popular belief, time doesn't slow down for you during a conflict; rather, your recollection of the event afterwards makes it feel this way).

The environment within which you are fighting and the sheer speed and force of your assailant's assault will often mean that the distance and space between you will get closed down and you will end up in each other's faces—having a complete control of range is more manageable before the fight begins, as opposed to while it is happening. At such close proximity, it is natural for both parties to try to grab and control each other, resulting in some form of a clinch scenario.

Defending Knees in a Clinch

One of the very real dangers of being caught in a clinch is having to deal with attacks made with the knees. Fortunately, most untrained individuals will throw their knees in a purely upwards fashion, rather than with any forward motion, which makes them easier to defend against. For a knee to be delivered with power, it really has to be thrown with the rear leg, meaning that an assailant has to step back before making an attack. To some extent, this telegraphs their attack and gives you forewarning as to which knee is going to be used. This is especially useful information if your attacker is throwing you around like a rag doll.

As soon as your head starts to come forward past your hips, you are in danger of being guillotined or having knees thrown in at you.

As your head comes forward, an assailant manages to get both hands to the back of your head and starts to pull you forward. At the same time, he steps back with his right leg to prepare for throwing a knee strike. Bring your hands up, ready to push them out to block the knee.

Knee strikes contain a lot of power, so you will need to do several things to negate this. Firstly, you must use the strength of both arms to make the block. Secondly, you must come to meet the strike before it gains full momentum.

Form one arm into a low 360 block and position the other across it in support. (See the close-up view at the end of the sequence on page 180 for correct positioning.) Drive your forearm into the oncoming leg as hard as you can. Push with the supporting arm and drive through the shoulders.

As soon as you have stopped the force of the attack, start to drop your elbow, and push across with your forearm, moving the assailant's leg outwards.

Continue this movement, forcing them to take a step to their right. This will open up their groin.

With your blocking arm, slap their groin.

Follow up with eye strikes, punches, elbows, knees, etc. before disengaging.

Close-up of arm/hand position—One arm makes a 360 Block using the forearm to drive into the attacker's quadriceps (upper thigh), while the other arm pushes down on the blocking arm to support it.

If your assailant is attacking with their right knee (you can predict this by watching them step back with their right foot), block with your right arm. If attacking with the left knee, then use your left arm.

Make a 360 Block with your right arm, making sure that the elbow is bent at a 90 degree angle. You should reinforce the arm by placing your other arm on top, with the fleshy underside of your supporting forearm against your blocking arm, pushing downwards.

As your assailant delivers their knee strike, use both arms to strike the blade of your forearm into their upper leg in an attacking fashion (you want them to associate every time they make a strike with receiving punishment).

After ramming your forearm into their leg, use your elbow to push their leg out, so they land in a wide stance. Now strike their groin, to start off an attacking combination.

Escaping a Clinch and Applying a Single Wing Choke

Although being in close to an opponent presents you with attacking opportunities that are not available at a longer range (such as throws, strangles, and chokes), being close also has its downsides if you are tied up with someone at such a range. For one, your visibility becomes seriously restricted, and this prevents you from gaining a full understanding of your environment (such as third parties who may be coming to assist your assailant, exit routes, objects you could use as improvised weapons, etc.). This is why it is important to either escape from the clinch quickly, or finish the person decisively using throws, strangles, chokes, or strikes.

When caught in a clinch, one of the first things you should try to do is gain control of your attacker's head—you can do this by establishing a high collar grip. Now you can use your forehead to drive into your assailant's eye socket, cheekbone, temple, etc. You are attempting to crush your aggressor's head between your forehead and arm. At the same time, lift your assailant's right arm at their elbow. Start to pull down on their head and drive with your forehead, so that you are forcing your aggressor's head toward the ground.

If you can throw them to the ground and disengage, you should do so. At the same time, scan around to assess other dangers that may be present, and objects within it you may be able to use to increase your chances of survival.

You may not always be able to drive your assailant completely to ground, so you might want to finish the fight conclusively with a choke or strangle. Use your forehead to cause enough pain that your aggressor's focus is diverted away from your hand on their elbow. Lift their elbow and duck underneath to come to their outside.

Pull your right arm back as you move from your opponent's side to their rear, and slide your left arm across their neck to grab their collar (or a handful of clothing around that area). Now slide your right arm behind their neck and under your left forearm. To apply a choke, simply straighten your arms and step back.

Move your assailant around and scan to gain a better understanding of your situation, then force them to the ground while choking them out.

If you end up in a clinch because you have been unable to control and maintain range, you are in a dangerous situation. If your assailant chooses to pull a knife at this point, the chances of them stabbing you are high; at the same time, if there are third parties in the locality who can assist your attacker, you won't be able to see them.

Immediately start to grind your forehead into your attacker's face, especially their eye socket. Pull the back of their head with your right arm as you do this, so they are unable to pull away from the pain.

Use this grinding action to direct their head downwards. At the same time, lift up their arm so you can step behind them.

Move all the way behind your assailant.

Keep your right arm around their neck to control them, and place your left hand, in a fist, at the bottom of their spine.

Push the base of their spine forwards, and pull backwards with the arm that is around their neck. This will take their balance, and if you are shorter than them, will also bring them down to a height where it is easier for you to deal with them.

While still pulling them back by the neck, remove your left hand from the base of their spine...

...And reach around the front of their neck to grab part of their clothing around the collar area (of whatever they are wearing) on the right side. At the same time, move your left arm to trap their right arm.

Try to grab some clothing as far behind their neck as possible. The deeper the clothing grab, the faster the choke will be applied. Your right arm should trap their upper right arm as you do this.

Raise your right hand up and slide it behind your assailant's neck.

As you do this, start to pull the clothing across/around your assailant's neck, first trapping and putting pressure on their right carotid artery...

...And then the left one. Straighten your left arm to increase the pull on the material, and your right, to put pressure on the back of the neck.

This photo shows the end position from the front. You can see how the t-shirt has been pulled round the neck to apply the choke. Chokes are a good way to finish a fight, especially against somebody who is impervious to pain—i.e., they are on drugs or drunk.

It is important to place the arm that is positioned behind the neck under your wrist. This prevents it slipping over your assailant's head.

Side Headlock Prevention

When dealing with inexperienced fighters, you will often find that they barrel forward, throwing punches, and are unable to control their movement and range—resulting in them jamming up against you. They may also try to defend themselves against your attacks by getting close and grabbing you, in order to avoid being hit. In both instances, you will often end up in a clinch, where your assailant will try to hold on to you, possibly controlling a limb as well as your head. Often, from the clinch position your assailant will try to apply a side headlock.

Your first awareness that a side headlock is being applied will be the sensation of a hand coming around your head and slipping behind the neck, with your assailant's arm putting downwards pressure on the back of your neck. As you feel this happen, your hand should immediately come up on the outside of their arm, and drive your palm into the side of your assailant's face.

As you do this, you should step back and to the side, making sure that your head is moved past the crook of the attacking elbow, toward their wrist. This hand and body defense will prevent you from being pulled both downwards and towards your attacker. Your other hand can be placed against their upper torso to help support your other arm and prevent them from pulling you towards them.

You should never wait for an attacker to put a hold or control fully in place before you attempt an escape. Likewise, for every hold/control you know, you should know how to prevent it from being applied.

In this situation, an attacker reaches round the back of your head to apply a side headlock hold/control. Immediately, you should start to reach your arm over theirs, and bring your other hand back to help prevent them from pulling you towards them.

With your left hand, put your fingers into their eyes and push them away. Put your other hand against their body and push away from them. You should try to move your head towards the wrist of their attacking arm—if they manage to get your head in the crook of their elbow, or closer to their shoulder, they will be able to pull you in and apply the lock.

Stepping back slightly, keep your fingers in their eyes pushing their head back. Pull your other hand away in preparation to strike them.

Set up your body to strike…

…And to turn towards your assailant, smashing your forearm into their neck.

Escaping a Side Headlock

If you are late in preventing a side headlock, which usually means you have not been able to move your head past the crook of your aggressor's elbow, you will find yourself being pulled forward. Hopefully, you will have already started to move your hands in the way described above to prevent the headlock in the first place, as you will be able to build on this movement in order to make the defense against the fully committed attack.

If your attacker responded to your rear strangle escape by pulling your head forward (or because you didn't turn your head in during your escape), you may end up with your head trapped under your assailant's armpit, and your chin caught on their forearm.

The biggest danger of the side headlock is not from being held and punched, but from being taken to the ground. There are certain occasions when it is an appropriate tactic to take the fight to the ground. However, these circumstances are limited, and as a general rule ending up on the floor is ill-advised, especially if you work off the assumption that your attacker may be armed and have third parties in the vicinity who can aid them (and this should always be your default assumption).

To prevent being taken to the ground, as you are being pulled forward, take a big step forward with your right leg—this should also help you get your hips back under your head. If you are able to shuffle/slide your left leg so it is behind your assailant's right leg, that is a bonus (but not essential).

As you make your step forward, your right hand should follow your right leg, so that as part of the same movement you can slap your attacker's groin. This is the same hand that was placed on the upper torso of your assailant as part of the prevention of the side headlock, so it should already be in front of your assailant's body.

The other hand, which was previously attempting to push against the side of your assailant's head, should now come over the shoulder and attack their eyes, making sure to avoid the mouth (so as not to be bitten).

In one movement, thrust the hips forward and stand up, cranking your assailant's head back by gouging the eyes. If you were able to place your left leg against the back of your aggressor's right leg, you can force your knee into the back of theirs, which will help to take them off balance, and so limit their resistance to your defense. From here, you should continue your attack.

This time, your attacker has managed to get you in a side headlock—they were able to pull you in and get your head under their upper arm. They will try to do one of two things from here: Either pull your head down in order to punch you; or take you to the ground.

As they pull you forwards, take a large step, so that you stay with them, rather than have them pull your head forward and past your hips. At the same time, bring your left hand up and over their right shoulder.

Combine the big step you take with a strike to your attacker's groin.

The groin strike should hit a little before your hand comes to your attacker's eyes. If they are taller than you, you will want the groin strike to hit, with the result that they bring their hips back and throw their head forwards. This will help your left hand reach their eyes.

Push your hips forward, stand up straight, and pull your attacker's head back by digging your fingers into their eyes.

Use the forearm that made the groin strike to smash into your assailant's neck.

After you have "softened up" your assailant with forearm strikes, place your right forearm under their chin and take a big step past them with your left foot. This should take your attacker off balance. You should be directing them so that all their weight goes onto their right leg.

Raise your right leg as high as you can...

...And then sweep it backwards, catching the back of your attacker's knee with your own.

Don't put your foot down, but continue to swing the leg upwards to lift your attacker's leg as high as you can.

Force them to the ground, and if possible make a hard strike against their ribs a moment after they land. When people hit the ground, they automatically exhale. At this point there is no air in the lungs, so the ribs lack the support that air in the lungs normally provides them. A timely strike now would break your attacker's ribs with relative ease.

Conclusion

There is more to protecting yourself than learning how to fight and defend yourself physically. Violence occurs along a timeline, with pre-violence indicators (PVIs), such as an assailant's synchronization of movement, which can alert you to the presence of danger; as well as victim facilitators (VFs), which are actions and behaviors you engage in that draw the attention of aggressors and predatory individuals. If you are able to learn how to reduce and eliminate these behaviors that draw attention to yourself, and understand how to identify those actions which an attacker needs to engage in before assaulting you, you will never need to use the techniques described in this book. This should be your goal.

Krav Maga was born out of the situation in which Israel found itself in the 1940s—and continues to find itself in today: outnumbered by enemies on all sides, as well as internally, who wanted to deny its existence. There are times when conflict is unavoidable—you may not be prepared to accept the consequences of not fighting. When such situations occur, you should work preemptively with full, unwavering commitment to your goal—ending the violence as quickly as possible.

If you do ever need to use the techniques described in this book, do so with everything that defines who you are, as every fight and confrontation you are involved in is a matter of survival, and you must meet it with every ounce of your emotional and physical being.

Acknowledgments

I would like to take this opportunity to thank Patrick Colin O'Reilly for his tireless work on photographing, editing, and helping select the final photographs for the book. His approach to capturing the movement of both attacker and defender has lead to a much more "realistic" work, than the one I first envisaged when I was approached to write the book. I would also like to thank Andy Rallings, for his technical contribution and advice (and continued support and friendship), as well as for his roles in portraying both assailant and target/victim in the photos. Other characters of note include Jake Augustern, Efe Atabay, Liz Berrien, Barry Bock, Sam Clark, Noah Grayson, Jeff Quigley, Jose Rodriguez, and Michael Ryan, for playing such convincing attackers and victims. I would also like to thank Justin Termini for helping us come up with the idea for the book's cover photo, and taking the numerous photos until we felt we had the right photo.

A big, big thanks to the owner and staff at Jenny's Pizza and Tavern at the End of the World in Charlestown, for allowing us to use their premises to shoot many of the scenarios described in the book. I would also like to extend my thanks to Scott Campeau, Dave Birringer, and Justin Termini for their editorial advice, input and tireless work in reviewing various iterations of the book, and to Liz Berrien for helping define and structure the book, as well as for her constant editing of it.

My biggest thanks go to all my instructors, who have taught me over the years. Especially to Marcos Lall (my first real Krav Maga instructor), who was the first person to really demonstrate the systematic nature of Krav Maga, and to Dennis Hanover, whose teaching and instruction influences almost everything I do.

OSS/Respect
Gershon Ben Keren

The Tuttle Story: "Books to Span the East and West"

Many people are surprised to learn that the world's largest publisher of books on Asia had its humble beginnings in the tiny American state of Vermont. The company's founder, Charles E. Tuttle, belonged to a New England family steeped in publishing.

Immediately after WW II, Tuttle served in Tokyo under General Douglas MacArthur and was tasked with reviving the Japanese publishing industry. He later founded the Charles E. Tuttle Publishing Company, which thrives today as one of the world's leading independent publishers.

Though a westerner, Tuttle was hugely instrumental in bringing a knowledge of Japan and Asia to a world hungry for information about the East. By the time of his death in 1993, Tuttle had published over 6,000 books on Asian culture, history and art—a legacy honored by the Japanese emperor with the "Order of the Sacred Treasure," the highest tribute Japan can bestow upon a non-Japanese.

With a backlist of 1,500 titles, Tuttle Publishing is more active today than at any time in its past—inspired by Charles Tuttle's core mission to publish fine books to span the East and West and provide a greater understanding of each.